Parenthood after 30?

Parenthood after 30?

A Guide to Personal Choice

Judith Blackfield Cohen
University of California

Lexington Books
D.C. Heath and Company/Lexington, Massachusetts/Toronto

Library of Congress Cataloging in Publication Data

Cohen, Judith Blackfield.
    Parenthood after 30?

    Includes bibliographical references and index.

    1. Parenthood. 2. Parenthood—Psychological aspects.
    3. Life cycle, Human. I. Title.
HQ755.8C64   1985   304.6'32   84–48826
ISBN 0–669–09844–2 (alk. paper)

Published simultaneously in Canada
Printed in the United States of America on acid-free paper
International Standard Book Number: 0–669–09844–2
Library of Congress Catalog Card Number: 84–48826

To all my parents

Contents

Figures and Tables

Figures

Tables

Self-Assessment Exercises

Preface and Acknowledgments

The purpose of this book is to help you explore a relatively new social option: considering parenthood later in the life cycle than has been usual during the course of history. For the first time, a large cohort of women and men has intentionally deferred not just parenthood but even making a final decision about parenthood for a decade or more past their twenties—the traditional age for beginning parenthood. By doing so, these people have been able to achieve, on the average, more education, career development, and personal growth than their peers who have become parents earlier. Sooner or later, however, they report that they feel pressure—from within, from family or friends, or just from their own "biological clock"—to make some decision.

This book addresses the various dimensions of the parenthood decision. It does not advocate either a pronatalist or a childless position; rather, it provides factual and experiential information on the physical, social, and psychological aspects of the decision-making process and compares possible alternatives for choice. Both the potential risks and the potential rewards associated with each alternative are presented because of the complexity involved in reaching this very personal decision.

Ambivalence is a significant part of the decision process, as is the timing dimension. Some people may be able to make a yes or no decision immediately but realize that their decision is not permanent and that they may need to reevaluate it in the future. Others may legitimately decide that no firm choice can be made at this time, but they may be able to specify the time and conditions under which reconsideration will be appropriate for them. Ultimately, of course, the biological clock limits the option to defer natural parenthood; still, many alternative parenthood roles are available, and they, too, are discussed here.

It is also important to recognize that few of us can unequivocally make a decision without some discomfort or second thoughts. Even those who feel certain now may not be so sure in a year or in five or ten years. It is also true, however, that human nature is surprisingly adaptable, even in this most personal of choices. Many people who would have chosen to become parents but could not or who chose not to become parents but had parenthood thrust upon them have proved to be capable of recognizing the positive aspects of their changed circumstances.

During the research for and preparation of this book, many people shared with me their knowledge, experience, concerns, and insights. Some were interviewed as individuals or couples; others participated in classes and seminars on reaching a decision about parenthood. Most of these people can be thanked only as a group, since they shared some of their most personal experiences with me with the understanding that they would not be identified as individuals.

Those whom I am able to thank individually are many, however, beginning with Lloyd Churgin, Director of Continuing Education in Public Health at the University of California, Berkeley, Extension Program, who encouraged me to start all this work. My thanks also go to Dr. Evelyn Bromet, Dr. Katherine Detre, Leslie Dunn, Dr. George Washington Hill, Martha Holstein, Judy MacLean, Carol Madore, Drs. Andrew Moss, Josefina Marin, Alex Rogerson, Lucy Scott, Judith Siegel, Aliyah Stein, Sandra Stein, Zena Stein, Joe Weick, Jerome Wolfson, and Norma Wikler. Ilana Schotz and Elfi Zanker helped me with research and clerical tasks, and I thank them especially for being there to help when my own energies were low. My "first editor," in many ways, Philip Cecchettini, motivated and sustained me, while providing an amazing variety of resource materials and leads for more; I feel fortunate to have made such a friend. Since then, I have been helped and encouraged by the editorial staff at Lexington Books, especially Kevin Ahern, Margaret Zusky, and Martha Cleary.

I have also been sustained by my personal support network; although we were often far apart, their encouragement was always there. Thank you Evelyn, Leigh, Margaret, and Sandra for materials and messages that helped in many ways. Finally, to those who have had to live with me for the duration, and who have provided encouragement and constructive criticism despite my varying ability to accept them, I owe the largest debt of all. Sam, Trudi, and Rebecca have taught me so much of what parenthood really means.

1
The New Choice: Parenthood as an Option

The Trend toward Deferred Parenthood

Parenthood as a "choice" is a relative novelty. Until recently in this country—and still in most of the world—parenthood has been a normal and expected part of the life cycle. The very few who were not parents were considered rare and unusual (such as the clergy) or simply unfortunate; fate, or the gods, or infirmity made parenthood impossible for them. For women, the concept of motherhood, if not considered their destiny, is certainly valued positively in all cultures, including our own; it is associated with images of warmth and caring, understanding and nurturing. For men, fatherhood includes the image of adult responsibility, a validation of their virility, and a continuity of the family line.

Most people still do not question the idea of parenthood for themselves, but contemporary circumstances permit the question to become one of "parenthood when?" Other plans—for completion of education, for personal and career development, and for financial security—make the decision to defer parenthood a reasonable one. Many people in their twenties feel that they still have a great deal to accomplish; their personal and career choices must still be made or developed. In addition, their personal, intimate relationships are often unstable, or at least untested. So time flies, and suddenly they are approaching age 30, 35, or even 40, and the old questions about parenthood take on new and urgent dimensions.

Although there have always been people who deferred parenthood voluntarily until later in life, until recently they have been rare exceptions. Throughout history, given the expectations of cultural norms and the uncertainty or lack of birth control alternatives, parenthood has predictably followed marriage within a few years. Both culture and technology are relevant factors here; a society that has effective birth control alternatives but still expects parenthood to be relatively prompt will show no change in the average age of parents at the birth of their first child. In the United States during the 1950s and 1960s, for example, there was no deferral of the initial age of parenthood, although total family size decreased. An interesting historical example of the reverse is the experience of many couples during the depression years of the 1930s, when parenthood was not considered such a good idea but birth control was much less available and reliable. Interviews with women married at that time who never had children reveal that, for them, a career (or keeping a job in those uncertain times) and parenthood were seen as mutually exclusive alternatives; by the time the country had climbed out of the depression, many of them had achieved some occupational prestige in a period that granted such status to women only rarely.[1]

During World War II, an unprecedented number of women who were also mothers went to work. It was recognized that the times were extraordinary, however, and child care arrangements were developed to a degree that has never again been achieved in this country. (The *New York Times* reported recently that there were fewer child care slots in 1983 than in 1945, although the number of working mothers was far greater.[2]) Even into the 1960s, cultural pressures in this country forced a separation between motherhood and occupational achievement. I recall sitting in a 1960 graduate seminar, "Sociology of the Family," at a prestigious university and watching the famous professor who taught the course driving an excellent but visibly pregnant student from the class with his remarks that women should not be in graduate school, that they would just have children and never work, and that they were wasting time and learning space that should be given to men.

Times have changed gradually; a more common recent stereotype has been the "supermom," who does it all—marriage, career, family, household—and outstandingly well at that. A large cohort of women who completed their education in the 1960s later made almost superhuman efforts to have careers and a family life without delaying or compromising either one. Most of these women married and began their families right after college, often helping their husbands complete advanced training as well. They tried very hard to be everything to everyone, but many found that they felt inadequate to the demands and that there was no "them" left to grow and be nurtured. The costs for such women and their families have been well documented.[3]

Another alternative has been chosen by more and more young adults recently. Observing the realities of establishing themselves personally, occupationally, and financially, they have chosen to defer the relative costs of establishing a family life temporarily, if not indefinitely. There are enough of such young adults that several changes in patterns of marriage have occurred in this country in the last decade.

First, although the number of marriages has continued to increase with increasing population, the rate of first marriages has declined, for two reasons. The most rapid population growth has been in the so-called baby-boom generation, but the marriage rate in that age group has actually declined. The rate of first marriages for unmarried women in that age group in 1980 was 103 per thousand women, a decrease of 5 percent from the 1979 rate and a 27 percent drop from the 1970 rate.[4] Even among those who do marry, there has been a clear trend in the last ten years toward older age at first marriage. By 1980, one-third of all women who had reached the age of 30 were still unmarried, a higher rate than at any time in our history.[5]

The second major change is the increasing proportion of marriages that are remarriages. By 1980, 44 percent of all marriages were remarriages of one or both partners, up from 31 percent in 1970. As table 1–1 shows, increases occurred in remarriage rates of both partners.[6]

There is also evidence that people not only are marrying later but also are delaying longer in starting families. Among women now in their late forties, nearly 70 percent had their first child before age 25; among women who are now in their early thirties, however, only 53 percent have had their first child.[7] Women in their thirties have the most rapidly rising rate of births of any age group, but this increased birthrate reflects a different pattern of timing than has been true in the previous generation. As figure 1–1 shows, there is now more delay between marriage and the birth of a first child and also between the births of the first and the second child. Only 33 percent of women married between 1970 and 1974 had babies during the first year of marriage, compared to 40 percent of women married ten years earlier.

Table 1–1
Percentage Distribution of Marriages by Marriage Order of Both Bride and Groom, 1970–1980

Year	All Marriages	First Marriage of Bride and Groom	First Marriage of Bride, Remarriage of Groom	Remarriage of Bride, First Marriage of Groom	Remarriage of Both Bride and Groom
1980	100.0	56.2	11.3	9.8	22.7
1979	100.0	56.4	11.2	9.5	22.9
1978	100.0	57.1	11.1	9.3	22.5
1977	100.0	57.5	10.8	9.0	22.6
1976	100.0	58.5	10.7	8.8	22.0
1975	100.0	60.1	9.9	8.6	21.3
1974	100.0	62.9	9.2	8.1	19.8
1973	100.0	64.6	8.7	7.9	18.9
1972	100.0	66.7	8.2	7.4	17.6
1971	100.0	67.7	8.0	7.3	17.0
1970	100.0	68.6	7.6	7.3	16.5

Source: National Center for Health Statistics, "Advance Report on Final Marriage Statistics, 1980," in *Monthly Vital Statistics Report,* DHHS Pub. No. (PHS)83-1120 (Hyattsville, Md.: U.S. Public Health Service, August 1983), p. 9.

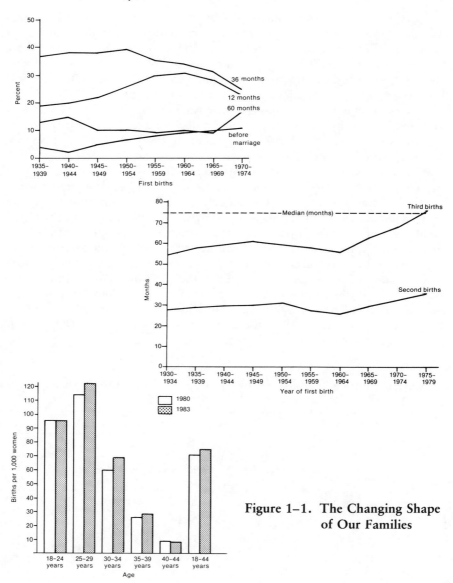

Figure 1–1. The Changing Shape
of Our Families

Similarly, of the later-marrying women, only 17 percent had a second child within three years, compared to nearly a third of the women who married earlier.[8]

Who are the people who are delaying both marriage and parenthood? It should not be surprising that the strongest association with this pattern is the extent of educational accomplishment and, associated with it, the ethnic and religious groups in which advanced education, especially for women as well as for men, is most pronounced. An example is provided by census and vital

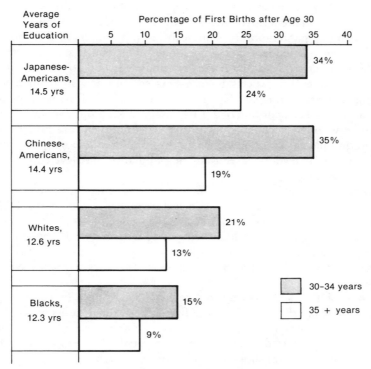

Source: National Center for Health Statistics, S. Taffel: Characteristics of Asian Births, United States, 1980. Monthly Vital Statistics Report, vol. 32 (10) supp. DHS Pub. No. (PHS) 84-1120, Feb. 10, 1984.

Figure 1–2. The Association between Educational Achievement and Older Parenthood, 1980

statistics reports on educational attainment and age at first birth of mothers from different ethnic groups in the United States (see figure 1–2). As of 1980, the ethnic groups with the highest averages of educational achievement are the Chinese-Americans and the Japanese-Americans; over 90 percent of these women have completed high school, and over one-third have completed college.[9] This is almost twice the proportion of white women who had completed college and over five times higher than the proportion of black women who had done so. As figure 1–2 shows, the percentage of first births to older mothers in each of these groups reflects the same gradient as their educational achievement. Among Asian-Americans, one mother of every five has her first child after age 35, compared to one of every nine among white mothers and one of every eleven black mothers. Over one-third of all first births to Asian-American mothers in 1980 were to mothers over age 30, compared to one-fifth of all births to white mothers, and about one-seventh of all births to black mothers.

The most extreme example of this pattern of higher educational achievement, professional employment, later or no marriage, and fewer or no children, is among contemporary American Jews. Members of this group traditionally have married later and have limited their family size more than their gentile counterparts, despite the religious dictum to "be fruitful and multiply." Recently, experts have estimated that Jewish women are now bearing an average of fewer than 1.7 children each per lifetime, far below the population replacement rate of 2.1 necessary to keep the population stable.[10] For these women, accomplishment and self-fulfillment are more important than traditional childrearing values, to the point that demographers and community religious leaders agree that the population has leveled off and may even be declining.

What is not yet clear is how many members of the "delaying" generation will change their minds. The Census Bureau has reported that, in 1980, nearly one in five women aged 30 to 45 was still childless.[11] The question is how many of them will be like their peers, who changed their minds later; between 1975 and 1979, there was a 73 percent increase in first births among women aged 30 to 35 and a 33 percent increase among women aged 35 to 39 years.[12]

These statistics reflect important new social trends. The current generation of women in their thirties is the first to have the benefits of reliable birth control technology; in addition, these women grew into adulthood during a period that emphasized everyone's right to personal development and choice in growth and accomplishment in life. During the years that they were in high school and college, the feminist movement became widespread and, among their generation, respectable. Educational equality and occupational equality became possibilities, if not accomplished realities. Probably more important was the shift in values that made personal accomplishment more important than making a good marriage at the right time. Parents and older relatives may have continued to ask a college graduate if she had found the right man, but the graduate was more concerned at the time with the right graduate school or career opportunity. These concerns were not temporary, either. Unlike their mothers, few women today expect to work only until they marry or until a husband's career is established.

If follows that people who defer marriage until they are more advanced in their own life course are more likely to be sure of who they are and what they want in life and to form friendships with others who have similar lifestyles and goals. Intimate relationships that grow from this life pattern tend to recognize the importance of each partner having the time and freedom to develop a talent, a professional career, or a satisfying occupational situation. Thus, emotional bonds can grow in a more balanced pattern of dependence and independence. The case for postponing a decision about parenthood is part of this pattern of mutually intended personal development and relationship building time. The delay time is another investment in the future, similar to the time spent in education and completion of training.

Many people who are still childless at age 30 or 35 assume that they will be parents "sometime," but for them, the issue of parenthood is becoming complicated by other developments. They are beginning to appreciate the advantages of the life they lead—not just occupational and financial security, but the freedom to indulge even whimsical impulses; these are not character-istics that they share with their friends of the same age who are parents. Also, although there are still many direct and subtle proparenthood messages around, these people may also be aware of a growing antiparenthood move-ment that supports them in their current childless state and even maintains that permanent childlessness is of value.[13]

There are people, however—in intimate relationships and not—who feel a strong pull toward parenthood but worry about the physical, genetic, or occupational risks of going ahead with parenthood at their age or in their pre-sent situation. By the time people have reached their thirties, they tend not to act on impulse, and they want relevant information to help them evaluate their options and risks before they make a decision.

Of course, everyone finds it helpful to have access to current information on all aspects of a decision that must be made. Available alternatives also must be evaluated in terms of personal experience and acceptability. How-ever, people facing this particular decision should be aware that a decision about parenthood can never be entirely rational—even with all the facts in the world—and that the process of reviewing factual information will not necessarily recognize or deal with the powerful but unrecognized feelings that can influence such a personal choice.

The process of delay itself builds a certain momentum that becomes hard to break. Time rushes by, and we keep our options open, but the "right" time—when careers, personal relations, and our own readiness can coin-cide—doesn't seem to be clear. It is easier to continue to delay and to avoid making a clear declaration of our intentions, waiting for that time when we can be sure of making the right decision. For many people in their thirties, what they call delaying parenthood is really delaying making a clear personal decision about parenthood. This delay is understandable; such a major deci-sion not only is terribly complex but also has disturbingly far-reaching reper-cussions. Furthermore, making a decision about parenthood is not just mak-ing a decision about the objective aspects of timing and arrangements; it also involves facing a series of intensely personal identity issues having to do with our own past and future. It may indeed be easier to avoid facing all this com-plexity, but to be uncertain for too long wastes time and energies that could be better used either for parenthood or for other kinds of valuable effort. Therefore, one purpose of this book is to help you move toward making the parenthood decision.

Components of the Parenthood Decision

The major components that enter into the parenthood decision—briefly introduced here—will be discussed in detail in the chapters that follow. Although they will first be presented separately, in reality they overlap in ways that are specific to each person who faces the parenthood decision. Strategies for integrating these components will be presented in the last chapter.

First, and most important, the parenthood choice is a personal decision. Although all aspects of your present lifestyle may appear to influence your decision and there is never a shortage of advisers, these external influences must ultimately be balanced within a deliberately subjective and personal perspective. For example, a person might have the most positive personal support and the most favorable occupational and financial circumstances but still be unable to imagine himself or herself as a parent; following honest self-examination, such a person might conclude that he or she has no interest in the parent role and is uncomfortable around children. (Please note that such people differ from those who are *uncertain* about how they would feel in the role of parent but are positive about exploring the uncertainty further, rather than disinclined to do so. Amateur status has never been a deterrent to parenthood.)

At another extreme is a person who feels strongly positive about parenthood despite personal or environmental circumstances that are not usually associated with successful family life. Some of these people do become parents—perhaps single parents or financially insecure parents—and some succeed very well as parents despite enormous difficulties. My position is not that those of you who may be in such circumstances should not choose parenthood but that you should be as well informed as possible about potential difficulties and about resources for coping with them.

For most people who are facing a decision about parenthood, the circumstances are not as extreme as those just presented. They feel positive about children and family life most of the time, and their personal, social, and economic circumstances are such that either a positive or a negative decision about parenthood seems possible. Their resources—interpersonal, developmental, and economic—can assume different orders of priority as they make the choice.

For many people, the primary issues are interpersonal. They may be relatively less concerned about occupational and financial adjustments and more uncertain about the potential effect of parenthood on their most important relationship. Both men and women fear that adding the demands of parenthood to a rich and complex relationship will inevitably diminish that relationship. Conversely, people who are uncertain about the stability of an intimate relationship fear to jeopardize it with the additional strains of parenthood. These concerns are often of primary importance to people whose first marriages did not work out and who are especially concerned about doing things right when they remarry. Others (not always women), who have hoped for an intimate relationship strong enough to support parenthood but have not found one, wonder if they should go ahead with parenthood anyway, as a single parent.

Each of these kinds of people has good reason to be concerned. A great deal of research has indicated that profound changes in relationships are to be expected with the advent of parenthood. However, the experts disagree about the nature and effects of these changes, especially among older parents. (Research findings will be discussed further in later chapters.)

Some people who are facing the decision about parenthood are more concerned about the potential effect of parenthood on the developmental gains they have worked so hard to achieve. Women particularly are aware of all the extra hours and the attention to details that have been necessary to accomplish what they have achieved so far; they have also seen the time and schedule conflicts of their co-workers who are parents—especially those who have young children. Cutting back on a career for a year or two may be economically feasible, but many professions have a knowledge base that changes so rapidly that time out means regression. Also, many women, especially professionals, have seen that the time taken for a much-desired pregnancy is viewed by their superiors as evidence of a lack of commitment to the profession. In a recent article stating why she is leaving academic medicine, a young physician quotes a well-publicized memo from a department chairman at Stanford Medical Center to a 30-year-old chief resident: "Your pregnancy is presumptuous and a disservice to your colleagues. . . . I am encouraged by other faculty to appoint no more women to the residency."[14]

Potential interruption of a work situation can also interrupt other important nonfinancial rewards. For many of us, some of our most important and supportive relationships are with friends at work—people who understand our job and personal problems and struggles and often figure in much of our recreational time as well. The value of such friendships in providing both instrumental and tangible psychological support is well recognized; it will be discussed in relation to parenthood changes in chapters 4 and 5.

For all these reasons, many potential parents would not choose to give up their career activities for as long as a year or more. Since many of their co-workers are also parents, they see their potential plans for parenthood as parallel rather than sequential to their work time. They may or may not be aware of how critically dependent their peers are on adequate child care arrangements, especially for emergencies such as late business meetings or a sick child. Given the huge gap between the present demand for quality child care and the limited resources available, many advisers (including experienced parents) suggest that potential parents arrange for child care even before becoming pregnant.

The final component of the parenthood decision involves that most personal and introspective level of questions for which there are no certain answers at the time a decision is to be made: What will happen to me if I become a parent—or if I never become one? Even if I feel sure now, will I be sorry about my decision in the future? For many people, these deepest concerns are intertwined with family experience. The two most common emotional themes of that experience—guilt and loss—are powerful ones. Writer and poet Adrienne Rich writes of when she first became a mother:

> But I was only at the beginning. Soon I would begin to understand the full weight and burden of maternal guilt, that daily, nightly, hourly, "Am I doing what is right: Am I doing too much? Am I doing enough?" The institution of motherhood finds all mothers more or less guilty of having failed their children; and my mother, in particular, had been expected to help create, according to my father's plan, the perfect daughter.[15]

Rich's mother's life also personified the other theme—loss. She had relinquished her own promising musical career, as well as all other "external" interests, for full-time parenthood, with sole responsibility for its implementation as well as its failure. Many feminist writers have now asked whether, given the current institutions of parenthood in this society, the price is not too high. The loss of self and the heavy weight of responsibility for another life are a formidable double burden.

However, many women and men who have waited until their thirties and forties to become parents also address the themes of loss and gain from the other side. One study that compared older parents to younger parents found that the older ones agreed that it was best to have waited—at least partly because they had time to develop personal relationships and identities that were independent of parenthood: "When you're set as a person and sure of your choices, you can appreciate the wonder of children growing in a way that you can't if you're still unformed yourselves."[16] Another study of women who had their first children or children of a second marriage after 35 reported that the new mothers often spoke of the late child as a "gift" and that they 'had more time," "felt more relaxed," and were able to appreciate "the absolute and unanticipated delight of this one" that only came with maturity.[17]

Attitudes toward the Parenthood Decision

Some apprehension and ambivalence are to be expected in the parenthood decision process. No choice with such profound effects on the rest of your life is likely to be simple or comfortable in the making. At this stage, people can be grouped according to three possible states of mind about the parenthood choice. The first can be described as uncertain but leaning in a positive direction. This group includes people who have always assumed that they would be parents "someday" and are asking whether now is the right time for them.

Another group, smaller in size but growing in numbers, includes those who are inclined toward a negative decision, but also with some uncertainty. This uncertainty may result from the increasing pressure of the "biological clock"; people in this group are not choosing parenthood at present, but they are concerned about how much longer they have to change their minds if they choose to do so. Other people are included in this negatively inclined group because of personal circumstances that are more lasting, such as a troubling family history of genetic or health problems or serious health problems of a spouse. Still others, though fairly sure that they are unenthusiastic about parenthood, are under pressure to join the ranks of parents; they are told that it is selfish, or childish, or abnormal not to become a parent.

Between these two groups is the largest group: those who would describe themselves as truly undecided. The complexity of the choice, with pressures in both positive and negative directions, does not allow them to feel part of either the positively inclined group or the negatively inclined group. This third group includes many different kinds of people, but for the purpose of working through the parenthood decision process, it will be useful to divide them into two subgroups: (1) those who are temporarily uncertain and feel that either additional information or a specific set of changed circumstances will permit them to leave the undecided group; and (2) those who feel that they may never be able to reach a firm decision but that the passage of time will, in effect, make the decision for them.

Conclusion

At this point, most readers will identify with one of the three attitude groups but will feel fairly tentative about their choice. Let me emphasize, again, that the purpose of this book is not to influence people to move into any of these choice positions but rather, first, to provide information in a framework that will permit assessment of the issues involved in making a decision about parenthood. In chapters 2 through 5, the potential changes and risks involved in the decision are presented, so that decision makers can come to grips with issues such as the following:

The medical and genetic risks (and myths) for people considering parenthood in their thirties and later.

The timing of parenthood (biological, adoptive, other), including child-spacing considerations.

The impact of parenthood on career.

The implications of parenthood for personal lifestyle.

The implications of parenthood for present and future family life and relationships with friends.

The role of personally important goals in the parenthood decision.

The second purpose of this book is to help readers move toward making a decision. Chapter 6 reviews the available decision alternatives, taking into account the timing dimension—that is, making a decision now versus making it at a specified future time. For each decision possibility and its attendant rewards and risks, the third purpose of the book is to provide support, both in discussion and in the resource materials, for further follow-up action on the decision that is made.

It is wonderful to have the opportunity to make a choice about parenthood, but it is difficult to know how to go about making the choice or to know whether the choice you make today will necessarily be the one you would want to live with in the future. Parenthood, once chosen, is irrevocable; you can't go back. On a less severe note, however, there is good evidence that the adaptability of human beings operates in this area, too; people who have become parents or remained childless without having made a deliberate decision to do so generally do quite well. Nevertheless, the process of working through a decision about parenthood can bring an awareness of the positive aspects of any of the possible outcomes as well as information about supportive resources.

Notes

1. See C.G. Heilbrun, *Reinventing Womanhood* (New York: Norton, 1979); L.C. Pogrebin, *Family Politics: Love and Power on an Intimate Frontier* (New York: McGraw-Hill, 1983), especially chapter 6, "Too Many Trade-offs: When Work and Family Clash," pp. 116–141.

2. *New York Times,* March 27, 1983.

3. See Pogrebin, *Family Politics:* E. Peck and Senderowitz (eds.), *Pronatalism: The Myth of Mom and Apple Pie* (New York: Crowell, 1974); R. Sidel, *Urban Survival: The World of Working Class Women* (Boston: Beacon Press, 1978); C. Bird, *The Two Paycheck Marriage* (New York: Rawson-Wage, 1979); J.H. Pleck, "The Work–Family Problem: Overloading the System," in B. Forisha and B. Goldsmith (eds.), *Outsiders on the Inside: Women and Organizations* (Englewood Cliffs, N.J.: Prentice-Hall, 1981).

4. National Center for Health Statistics, "Advance Report on Final Marriage Statistics, 1980, " in *Monthly Vital Statistics Report,* DHHS Pub. No. (PHS)83–1120 (Hyattsville, Md.: U.S. Public Health Service, August 1983).

5. Bureau of the Census, *Childspacing Among Birth Cohorts of American Women, 1905–1959* (Washington, D.C.: U.S. Department of Commerce, April 1984).

6. National Center for Health Statistics, "Advance Report."

7. S.J. Ventura, "Trends in First Births to Older Mothers, 1970–79," in *Monthly Vital Statistics Report,* DHHS Pub. No. (PHS)82-1120 (Hyattsville, Md.: U.S. Public Health Service, May 1982).

8. Bureau of the Census, *Childspacing.*

9. S. Taffel, "Characteristics of Asian Births, United States, 1980," in *Monthly Vital Statistics Report,* DHHS Pub. No. (PHS)84-1120 (Hyattsville, Md.: U.S. Public Health Service, February 1984).

10. *Wall Street Journal,* April 13 and 23, 1984.

11. Bureau of the Census, *Childspacing.*

12. Ventura, "Trends in First Births."

13. D. Burgwyn, *Marriage Without Children* (New York: Rawson-Wade, 1981); M. Faux, *Childless by Choice: Choosing Childlessness in the 1980's* (Garden City, N.Y.: Anchor Press/Doubleday, 1984).

14. D.M. Barnes, "First Person," *San Francisco Examiner and Chronicle,* June 10, 1984.

15. A. Rich, *Of Woman Born: Motherhood as Experience and Institution* (New York: Norton, 1976), p. 223.

16. P. Daniels and K. Weingarten, *Sooner or Later: The Timing of Parenthood in Adult Lives* (New York: Norton, 1982).

17. I. Kern, "No Better Time: The Choice of Parenting After 35," Paper presented at the National Association of Social Workers Professional Symposium, Washington D.C., November 22, 1983.

2
Why People Delay Facing the Parenthood Decision

The Delaying Process

As used here, the term *delay* includes several stages of a process that begins with the awareness that you are considering parenthood or nonparenthood and ends with definite action on your part to carry out the decision you have made. People in the early stages tend to make such statements as "I hadn't really thought about it one way or another until recently." They may be in their thirties or older, but they have been busy with other aspects of their lives that have precluded the personal circumstances appropriate for such reflection. For example, a 35-year-old woman said to me:

> I haven't been delaying making a decision—until a few months ago. I had no urge to settle down, and hadn't met anyone I wanted to settle down with until then. We married later than most of our friends, and we're glad we did. Now is the right time for us to start thinking about kids, but we didn't marry each other just to automatically start a family like a lot of younger people seem to do.

An intermediate stage of the delaying process is characteristic of most people who are having difficulty making a decision about parenthood. They usually are trying to decide whether parenthood is right or wrong for them in a mixed personal context, with some influences toward parenthood and other concerns that make them feel hesitant or cautious about it. A later section of this chapter provides several brief case descriptions of such people who are delaying coming to a definite decision, pro or con.

The last stage of the delaying process is when a decision has been made but there is a delay in acting upon it. Many people who are at this stage claim that they plan to become parents but are not sure of the right time in their lives to go ahead. As Daniels and Weingarten have pointed out, these "parents, sometime" may find themselves in the nonparent group by waiting too long for an ideal time that never comes.[1] However, the people at this stage also include those who are not as sure as they would like to be about their decision and want to keep other options open. Finally, perhaps the most unfortunate people who find themselves at this stage are those whose commitments either way are strong but whose partners disagree and those whose circumstances, such as being single, make it nearly impossible for them to act on their decision.

Facing Up to the Unknown

People delay making decisions and acting upon them for all sorts of reasons. The more important the impact of the decision will be on their lives, the more reasons they are able to find to delay even the process of working through to a decision-making point. Any change from the familiar and the established carries some element of risk, even if the existing situation is not entirely comfortable. The decision about parenthood is considered a major one by many people, and more and more people in their twenties and thirties who have no children are unwilling either to declare themselves permanently childless or to make a decision to go ahead and have children. They may be evasive, uncertain, or ambivalent about the choice, but, in any case, delay is easier for them than decision.

For people who are comfortable with delay and recognize little internal or social pressure to make a decision, there will of course be little impetus to move toward a decision—or even to read materials such as this book. It is likely, however, that many delaying adults, both men and women, are uncomfortable about a major decision that includes so many sensitive aspects of personal experience, self-image, and future hopes and fears.

Exercise 1 provides some examples of the typical concerns people have about facing the parenthood decision. Try the exercise yourself and then, if possible, compare notes with your partner or with others who are facing the same decision.

All of the statements in Exercise 1 are legitimate concerns for some people who are delaying, but they are not reasons to continue delaying indefinitely. If your response to most of them is "Delay more," you may well be unable to face making a choice about parenthood at this time, regardless of the details of your situation. (We will return to why this may be so later). If, however, you respond to most items with either "Yes (go ahead)" or "No (no reason to decide)," you have the first step toward decision making. This first step includes deciding what issues are relevant in understanding your own delay and how important each of the issues is in your own decision process.

In addition to the contextual or situational issues in Exercise 1, there is an additional, crucial assessment for you to make here: what you consider to be the meaning of *parenthood*. The statements in Exercise 2 are designed to

Exercise 1
Facing the Parenthood Decision

Read each of the following statements and choose the response that you think is the best course of action.

Yes (go ahead with parenthood) *Delay more* *No* (no reason to decide to have a child)

_____ All along, I lived out the expectations that I thought others had for me—for example, choosing a career, living a certain lifestyle—but I never asked myself what I really wanted. Now I am ready to give myself what I want—a family.

_____ I was worried that having babies might end my freedom, but now I am less concerned about that.

_____ I thought a perfect relationship was the prerequisite for starting the ideal family, but I am not so sure anymore whether there is such a thing as a perfect relationship.

_____ I kept postponing having babies because I was worried that it might be detrimental to my career, but my career isn't moving as fast as I had hoped.

_____ I thought my career would fulfill me, but now I realize that it can never give me the same emotional satisfaction as having a kid of my own.

_____ (Women) I always said that the father of my child would have to be prepared to share equally in the childrearing responsibilities, but now I am not so sure whether that is too much to hope for.

_____ (Men) I always believed that a mother should stay at home with young children, but that will not be possible for my wife.

Exercise 2
The Pros and Cons of Parenthood

Consider how strongly you agree or disagree with each of the following statements about parenthood. (There is no right or wrong answers.)

Disagree   *Agree*

├──┼──┼── A primary reason for our existence is to continue the human race in the best possible way. ──┼──┼──┤

├──┼──┼── Children make you feel important. ──┼──┼──┤

├──┼──┼── Becoming a parent is costly in terms of achieving other personal goals. ──┼──┼──┤

├──┼──┼── Being a parent makes you more realistic and responsible. ──┼──┼──┤

├──┼──┼── Children make you a more loving person. ──┼──┼──┤

├──┼──┼── Parenthood means the end of flexibility and freedom in most things. ──┼──┼──┤

Exercise 2 continued

Disagree		*Agree*
├─┼─┼─	Children give you a feeling of success and accomplishment.	─┼─┼─┤
├─┼─┼─	Parents of small children are boring because they only talk about their babies (or have no other interests but their babies).	─┼─┼─┤
├─┼─┼─	Parenthood strengthens the bonds between the parents.	─┼─┼─┤
├─┼─┼─	Even if you feel good now about not having children, you will regret that decision when you are old.	─┼─┼─┤
├─┼─┼─	Being a parent is one of the most creative and rewarding experiences.	─┼─┼─┤
├─┼─┼─	Whatever dreams did not come true for you, you will have another chance to experience your dreams through your children.	─┼─┼─┤
├─┼─┼─	Most marriages fall apart when the children are young.	─┼─┼─┤
├─┼─┼─	People should become parents when they are young enough to keep up with the demands of parenthood.	─┼─┼─┤
├─┼─┼─	You lose your youth and playfulness once you accept the enormous responsibilities of parenthood.	─┼─┼─┤
├─┼─┼─	People who never become parents miss experiencing some of life's richest times.	─┼─┼─┤
├─┼─┼─	You cannot develop your full potentials without having had children.	─┼─┼─┤
├─┼─┼─	Parenthood is a very heavy financial burden.	─┼─┼─┤
├─┼─┼─	Children keep you young and involved.	─┼─┼─┤
├─┼─┼─	Parenthood is repetitive, messy, and demanding, with no guaranteed rewards.	─┼─┼─┤
├─┼─┼─	You cannot be totally happy and fulfilled without a family of your own.	─┼─┼─┤

help you explore the many aspects of parenthood. All of the statements are true to some extent. Although some of them may appear to be entirely positive or entirely negative, further consideration will demonstrate that each contains some positive and negative elements; aspects of parenthood that appeal to one person may be the least desirable aspects to another. If your mate or partner is also working through this decision, each of you should complete the exercise separately. If there are major differences in your reactions to some of the statements, the discrepancies may help you understand how your views of parenthood differ and whether those differences are affecting your decision making as a couple.

Although parenthood has many aspects, the themes that occur most often in discussions about it can be grouped into two categories: rewards and responsibilities. On any given day, the role of parent is some combination of these categories. If you see parenthood as entirely one or the other, your view is probably unrealistic in terms of survival as a successful parent.

If you agreed with most of the statements about parenthood in Exercise 2, chances are that you already see the role of parent realistically, as a mixture of demands and delights. The one statement that is not supported by either research or experience is the judgment that "younger is better" where parenthood is concerned. On the contrary, a great deal of evidence indicates that older parents tend to be more satisfied and successful in their new parent roles than people who become parents at earlier ages. Older parents more often report that they feel that they have made the right choice at a time in their lives when they have accomplished more and are more certain of their own ability and experience in making decisions. They have accepted the responsibilities as well as the rewards in their transition to parenthood.

Although most people say that they delay making a choice about parenthood because of their concern about the responsibilities involved, they are making this assessment in a specific context. Each of us is part of a web of roles and relationships, each with its own rewards and responsibilities. Although some people cannot see anything positive about parenthood in any context, for most of us, parenthood is best considered both as part of and additional to our existing personal context. The personal decision-making environment for each person is unique, but some common patterns in the case description that follow may be familiar to you.

Case Examples: People Who Are Delaying

Eleanor and Don: Leaning away from Parenthood, but . . .

Eleanor, 33, and Don, 35,[a] have lived together for several years; neither has ever been married. They describe their relationship as exciting and rewarding, although they lead relatively independent lives. Eleanor has advanced to a senior administrative level in the large company for which she works, while

---

[a]The case examples used in this and subsequent chapters come from information provided by men and women who have participated in my research or in university courses I have taught. Since the information was volunteered in a context that promised them anonymity, I have changed identifying information such as names and locations. The examples have been chosen because they are typical of the situations or experiences of many people who are facing a decision about parenthood.

Don has moved among several creative jobs. They both take pride in their respective accomplishments and like the freedom and flexibility in their life together.

At present, they describe themselves as leaning away from parenthood, but they are unwilling to state that they have made a final decision. Their families and others still pressure them at times about "growing up"—that is, settling down and getting on with the "real" part of life, parenthood. Don remembers his own family as warm and positive, and wonders whether he is being somewhat selfish in continuing his present ways. He also wonders whether he will be sorry when he is older if he has no family to share his life. Eleanor says she receives even more pressure to settle down, but her own childhood memories are not very positive. She remembers the burdens and the unhappiness of her mother's responsibilities more than the rewards, and she is concerned that Don might follow the path that her father and other men often take—pursuing his own opportunities for creative growth and leaving her with most of the family responsibility. Yet she does not see herself or want to be seen as cold and nonnurturing. Indeed, she describes her relationship with Don as still romantic and intense, and she wonders whether they really have room in their intimate life for the additional demands of a child. She observes that she knows some women who combine a good relationship with a good career, but she knows no one who has both of these and still feels that she is a good mother.

Janet and Tom: Deferral Made Sense, but Is It Too Late Now?

Janet and Tom married in their mid-twenties, when she was already a practicing professional and he was completing his specialty training. They are now in their mid-thirties and express surprise that the intervening years have rushed by so rapidly. They report, however, that they have delayed making a decision about parenthood only recently. In their early years together, they just assumed that they would become parents "someday," when their careers were more developed and their financial situation was improved. To them, parenthood has always had a positive meaning, but they are also serious about the many responsibilities it entails.[2] Recently, however, Tom and Janet have become more aware of the contrast between their lives and those of their peers who are parents. The freedom to stay late to work on a job task or to travel to business meetings and for pleasure has become something that they take for granted as part of their lives. They have the flexibility to be available if something comes up on short notice, and they are aware that such flexibility has served them well in both career and recreational situations. They are also aware that their friends who are parents do not have nearly the same degree of freedom or flexibility, especially when their children are young; and even those whose kids are older have less financial freedom. Janet says that they would like to continue as they are for a while longer, but she fears that, for her, the biological clock may be running out. She is aware of the possibility of increased risks of pregnancy problems and of birth defects in children born to older mothers. Tom adds a longer-range concern—the responsibility for college-aged offspring when he will be facing the reduced income that accompanies retirement. Although they still feel that parenthood would be good for them, Janet and Tom wonder whether they have already waited too long to start a family.

Diane and David: Personal Uncertainty Affects the Decision

Diane, 35, has been living with David, 40, for two years, and their friendship goes back several years before that. Their intimate relationship has had its ups and downs, but they both describe it as more positive than not, and they feel that they have worked through some major differences. Both of them come from working-class backgrounds and have had to work hard to achieve their current levels of accomplishment and their comfortable lifestyle. Diane, especially, is regarded as unusually successful by her large family; she is the only one to have completed college and achieved success in the working world. It is this success that has led to Diane's perception that she is something of an outsider in her own family. Although she still wants children of her own, she sees that her sisters have grown to be much like her mother, trying to balance nurturing and the extra work schedule necessary to pay family bills and struggling to raise their families right with little support from their spouses, who work hard, too, but regard parenthood as women's work.

David is not unsympathetic, but he doesn't share her sense of dilemma. He already has a child from a previous marriage and would be content to have no more children. However, if Diane wants children, he'll go along with it. Diane rightly fears that his attitude is not likely to lead to a strong commitment to the kind of egalitarian parenthood she desires.

Anne: Single Parenthood May Be the Only Available Choice

Anne, approaching 40, can take pride in a professional career path of accomplishment. She notes ruefully, however, that this success has not been compatible with the caliber of sustained and rewarding intimate relationship she considered necessary to begin the family she also would have liked to have. Lately, she has begun to wonder more and more frequently about the possibility of going ahead with single parenthood, rather than settling for parenthood in a less than optimal relationship or no parenthood at all. Her career, once so exciting, has reached a sort of plateau, and there is not as much to look forward to as there had been. She is sure that her work could be managed successfully part-time, and she has even thought about letting her career take an entirely new turn, with or without parenthood.

Anne describes herself as someone who has achieved a great deal of personal growth and who now likes her independent self and is confident in her judgment and abilities. Recently, she has also begun to discover an increased sensitivity to herself and others as part of her maturing. She is sure that as a more mature person, she is now ready to be nurturing and sensitive to the needs of a child. Earlier in her life, she would not have had the flexibility, patience, or sense of humor that she believes are essential aspects of successful parenthood.

Anne has seen friends and co-workers having a hard time as single parents, but she notes that she has also seen those who are in difficult marriages experiencing even more strain as parents. She says that friends can be at least as emotionally supportive and helpful as husbands. She also believes she could generate enough income, even from part-time work, to pay for child care. Still, she has many concerns: How much of her parenthood urge is a result of career staleness, and how much is a sense of panic because she feels that time is running out for her? How will she actually go about becoming pregnant if she decides to do so? If she does go ahead, will she regret her decision in a decade, when she is nearing 50 and has a son or daughter who is only 10?[3]

Susan and Steven: Different Role Definitions

Susan, 33, and Steven, 35, have been married for one year. They met at the university, both having returned to school to acquire new skills for pursuing their careers. Susan had been moving from job to job since her early twenties, and only in the past few years has she been able to identify a career path that she feels would be fulfilling for her. Steven had felt that he needed further academic work to move ahead in his field, to which he is very dedicated. They both face additional years of classwork and internships before they will be ready to enter higher-status positions. For both of them, their decision to commit themselves to additional schooling was made with the knowledge that they wanted children but had not found the right partner; so they decided to invest their time in their studies. At this point, Susan feels that if she were to take time off right after graduation, she would be losing all the time she has already invested and would return to her previous situation of no established career path. They both are concerned about financial stability and the indebtedness they have incurred for their studies. In their discussions of these dilemmas, they have also noticed that they have different definitions of the role of parent. Susan considers the ideal situation for her to be co-parenting—sharing child care time equally and working in part-time positions. Having been raised in a home where both parents worked, she feels that it is best for children to spend a great deal of time with both parents. She also feels that the stresses of parenting are eased when both parents share the responsibilities, and that co-parenting would enable her to progress, albeit more slowly, in her profession. Although he would want to spend time with his children, Steven does not feel comfortable with the lifestyle sacrifices they would have to make if he were not working full-time. He has grown accustomed to and comfortable with the way they live, and he is looking forward to moving ahead again on his career ladder. He is afraid of the sense of deprivation he might feel if he only worked part-time when all his colleagues were making full-time progress in their careers and receiving the attendant benefits.

Mary and Jeff: When Readiness Occurs at Different Times

Mary, a 32-year-old occupational therapist, has been married to Jeff, a 27-year-old lawyer, for nearly two years. They met while working as volunteers on a political campaign. At first, Mary's friends kidded her about being involved with a younger man. She points out, however, that they share many interests and activities, and she really likes his openness and sensitivity, which is so different from the self-interested distance of the older men she has been involved with in the past. Mary and Jeff tend to spend their nonwork time quietly with each other, and they prefer to be outdoors whenever possible. They describe themselves as more like "an old married couple than most of the married couples we know."

With regard to parenthood, each reports feeling positive about the role of parent, and each is also sure that the other would make an ideal co-parent. Their one fundamental difference concerns the timing or readiness for parenthood. Mary says:

> I never felt ready for motherhood until now, for a number of reasons. Probably my work had something to do with it; I worked my way through school and had no time for a social life. Also, I'm more shy than average, so my social life even since then hasn't been much to speak of. Only recently I've begun to feel sure of myself and who I am and what I want for the rest of my life. Of course, there had never been anyone like Jeff in my life until now either. We have a secure, positive relationship that is ideal for children, and I'm ready for them. Further, time won't be getting any better for me in terms of risks medically, so why delay further?

Jeff sounds somewhat defensive when he tries to explain why he does not feel ready to be a parent now:

> I like kids, and I'd like to have some of my own, someday. I'm sure that Mary would make a terrific mom but I'm just not able yet to see myself as a dad. My job includes travel, and I don't want to change my work now or cut back—my promotion to this level is new and exciting and it's important to me to stay involved with it now. I'd feel guilty and torn being a parent and gone so much. And we have so many other things to do now—we're buying a little cabin in the mountains, and it'll take lots of fixing up before we could take a baby up there. Frankly, I feel like I'm damned if I do and damned if I don't about this parenthood business right now!

Sally and Frank: A Family History Concern

Sally and Frank met and married in their late twenties; each of them had been married before. Neither of them had felt secure enough in their previous relationships to consider becoming parents, but now they are facing what appears to them to be a difficult and painful decision about starting their own family. Sally, an only child, is uncertain about her potential role of parent; although she likes children, full responsibility for a child seems like a great deal to take on, and babies are especially intimidating. Their major concern, however, is Frank's family history. He has a much younger sister who is severely handicapped and mentally retarded, and they fear that he may pass this problem along to a child of theirs. Frank's memories are vivid of the severe emotional and financial strain his younger sister's existence placed on his parents and on the other children in the family. Sally and Frank have even considered adoption, but they have not explored it further because they have heard about the scarcity of adoptable babies and the long waiting period involved; they also doubt that they would be young enough, in their mid-thirties, to be eligible. They have read about artificial insemination, but they confess that it makes them uncomfortable to talk about it, and they are sure that their families would be horrified if they went ahead with this option.

Ways of Dealing with the Potential Risks of a Decision

Purposive Delay

Many of the delay situations described in the foregoing case examples can be characterized as purposive delay. The basic pattern is to delay *until* something has been tested or accomplished. Since the widespread availability of contraception, some purposive delay has been the norm, even for couples who wholeheartedly advocate and desire parenthood. The boundary between brief and prolonged delay is not hard and fast, even to the couples involved; in general, the difference can be seen in their description of the extent and magnitude of the purpose for the delay. Thus, people who say that they are delaying only until some specific goal has been reached are usually able to make a choice about parenthood. In contrast, those who say that they are delaying—usually for an unspecified time—until they progress in their career development or achieve more personal growth through exploration and self-awareness are usually having more difficulty making the choice.

These kinds of vague but purposive delays occur, in part, because it is difficult to be specific about such goals. It is also difficult, however, to predict where or when one may end such a delay with regard to the parenthood decision. For many people, the reasons for delays may themselves be in conflict with a personal image of parenthood. The paths of growth, development, or personal accomplishment are engrossing and energy-consuming, but so is parenthood. People who are devoted to any pursuit to the degree that it takes up all their available time and energy are not likely to take on a new major role; or if they do, they are not likely to succeed at it to their satisfaction.

Conditional Delay

A somewhat different aspect of delay in making a choice about parenthood includes the reasons people give for delaying *unless* something occurs, rather than *until* it occurs. In this case, the delay is caused by the absence of some level of security that is necessary to make a decision; only when this security is present can the decision be faced. The most frequent version of this kind of delay is interpersonal. Recall that Anne could not consider parenthood unless she found a partner relationship of a quality that met her standards. Many women, especially, report that they are delaying consideration of parenthood unless they have the right relationship or a more stable one than they presently have.

Unfortunately, since it is usually impossible to fit either a specific time-table or specific tasks to these "unless" situations, they may continue unresolved for an indefinite period. Lack of clarity in knowing just what is wanted makes it even more difficult to know how to proceed, even if one or both partners want to try. Peope seem to find it easier to specify what they lack in such situations than to be clear about what they want or would be willing to settle for.

A related and pervasive issue for many men and women who are delaying the parenthood decision emerges in several forms from the case examples given here. For example, Eleanor's childhood memories were of her mother's burdens and responsibilities of parenthood. Furthermore, she was concerned that of their two careers, only Don's was likely to continue to grow and be flexible in the face of parenthood, and that she might be left carrying the full load of parenting time and energy and also the potential guilt and self-blame. Diane, too, comes from a cultural and economic family background in which motherhood is expected in addition to work, if necessary, but in which fatherhood means providing financial security to the family but not sharing parenting time and tasks. She has managed, largely through her own efforts, to achieve a work status that is more of a career—that is, increasing commitment and responsibility but also increased status, prestige, and income. It is understandable that she would be concerned that these gains might be compromised by a more traditional parenting pattern.[4]

Many women perceive their mothers to have been second-class citizens in a male-dominated society—lacking in self-esteem and claiming "only" the roles of housewife and mother, with little opportunity to develop themselves in other directions. Daughters of such mothers are understandably more likely to defer or deny parenthood, thus hoping (often unconsciously) to fulfill their mothers' unrealized dreams through their own achievements. Many daughters report that their mothers told them that if circumstances had permitted, they, too, would have chosen a childless life.[5]

For many couples who delay making a choice about parenthood, this role issue is an unresolved part of that delay. Such statements as "He has to want a child as much as I do" indicate a continuing difference between partners regarding the commitment to parenthood, with all its demands on time and energy. Traditionally, when child care was women's work, parents did not have to "want" parenthood equally. Now, many couples have succeeded in achieving more balanced relationships, in which the wishes, goals, and autonomy of each partner are recognized as being of equal value. Such relationships are easier to establish and maintain, however, when the couples are childless. On the basis of their personal experience and their observations of friends, many women fear that this equality will break down in the face of the demands of parenthood.[6]

Many men remember their fathers primarily as providers for the family larder, rarely available to play an active parenting role. Sons of such fathers find it difficult to imagine themselves in a more active and involved parent role, despite changes in social expectations. They support the choice of their partner to have a child if and when she wishes, but they have mixed feelings about whether the child should change their own lifestyle very much.

There are also many men who are more enthusiastic than their partners about the prospect of parenthood and who believe that they should play a very active role in parenting. Even these men, however, express concern about how they will translate this ideal into a day-to-day operation. They have no experience and no role models to follow; thus, they, too, have difficulty trying to consider parenthood as a potential part of their lives.[7]

Avoidance Because of Fear

Although they are more rare, some of the deepest reasons for avoiding the choice about parenthood are those dictated by fear. A significant minority of adults are terrified of pregnancy or childbirth, not just as a painful and disruptive experience, but as one that has led to permanent damage or death within their personal experience. Such fears may be so powerful that medical reassurance about their lack of validity may not even be sought or, if provided, may not be believed. Another major fear is that they may be passing on a serious physical or mental defect. People with family histories of major psychiatric disorders may feel so stigmatized that they do not even seek out the details of the family history and often do not share the information they have with their partners. Current diagnostic and counseling resources can be of significant help for people facing such problems, but only if the problem has been admitted and faced by the couple as part of the parenthood decision. If that recognition is too painful, the delay in making a decision about parenthood may be prolonged to the point where the relationship suffers or there is no longer a biological possibility of parenthood.

Identifying the Reasons for Delay

The case examples presented here may have highlighted many of the issues you are grappling with in facing the parenthood decision. At this point, it may be helpful for you to identify, as clearly as possible, which factors are involved in your decision, what you need to know or accomplish before you can decide, and when you expect to have a clearer sense of your situation. Use Exercise 3 as a reference, paying special attention to items that seem vague or for which you cannot identify a specific endpoint. If it is difficult for you to fill in columns B and C right now, keep them in mind and complete them as you proceed through the book.

Exercise 3
Identifying Your Reasons for Delaying the Parenthood Decision

Column A: *Issues re parenthood*	Column B: *What do you need to know or have happen for resolution?*	Column C: *When do you expect resolution?*
My first major issue is:		
Another issue for me is:		
Another issue for me is:		

Needless to say, it is unusual for only one of the foregoing reasons to serve as the full explanation for delay in making a choice about parenthood. More often, various combinations of these contingencies go into creating what is, for many people, a semipermanent state of avoiding a decision. They assess their current lives (busy, changing), their achievement (incomplete), their financial situation (inadequate), and their relationship (unavailable, or unpredictable, or unsatisfying, or not sufficiently supportive) and conclude that they will feel more positive about making a decision "when the time is right," rather than as things are now. They are more certain of when the time is not right, however, than they are of when or under what conditions the time *will* be right for them.

To the extent that both partners agree that the time is not right and are identifying the same factors to be addressed so that a "right" time is possible, this delaying strategy is both realistic and effective. Among some couples, however, the position that the present time is not right may be taken by only one partner and may cause dissension and frustration in the relationship. Traditionally, this was the male partner's strategy when his mate wanted children; recently, however, increasing numbers of couples report that the woman is the delaying partner. If you accept the view of some political analysts of family life—that it is the partner with the most to lose who takes this delaying position—then it is reasonable to expect that more women may be delaying because of their newly won positions of freedom and prestige.[8] News reporter Betty Rollin once observed that part of the myth of motherhood is that the production of a baby is the biggest accomplishment of a woman's life, but if that is so, it doesn't say much for the rest of her life.[9]

A conflict between partners about delay may, however, be a reflection of fundamentally opposed attitudes toward parenthood. If it appears that there never will be a "right" time for one of the partners, then each partner must assess the importance of his or her parenthood position in relation to the importance of the relationship itself. Major work on common goals in the relationship may be necessary. Some couples prefer to avoid the strain of facing these fundamental differences, so they may mutually avoid being forced to a parenthood decision that can have severe consequences for their relationship.

Experts agree that having children cannot save a relationship that is faltering. Furthermore, children born into such a relationship will bear some of the costs of current and future dissension. Especially for the sake of those who do not ask to be born, parenthood should not be seen as either inevitable or obligatory. If there are substantial doubts, delay is the preferable choice.

The Timing Dimension

Finally, it is appropriate to clarify the concept of the "right" time for reaching a decision on parenthood. Clearly, there are better and worse times for facing decisions of any kind; however, by universal standards, there is no single definition of a time that is completely and unambiguously right for any person. People who insist on waiting until the time is completely right will probably never go ahead with parenthood, although they may become de facto nonparents if they wait long enough. Conversely, many people, for reasons that are not entirely clear even to them, decide rather suddenly, regardless of circumstances, that the right time has come for them to make a decision. The materials in this book may help to address this timing issue in several ways. For some readers, clarification of the dimensions of their delay will make it possible for them to reach a decision and organize available resources to act on that decision and deal with its consequences. For others, agreement can be reached on the issues to be resolved or the goals to be accomplished so that they can wait for a better time to face a decision or reevaluate their situation.

Since many women, especially, feel pressured to make a decision before they are ready because their "biological clock" is ticking, the information on medical and genetic risk in the next chapter can provide reassurance that this biological pressure need not be inexorable.

Conclusion

The generation of people now in their thirties is unusual in the diversity of choices and the freedom to choose among them that have become available during the last two decades. Living in a country where economic growth has been strong and educational and occupational opportunities have never been greater, the complexity of deciding how to live one's life has grown accordingly. As most have discovered by now, more freedom of choice means more effort and responsibility in making decisions and living with their consequences. There are few guidelines from prior generations, whose realities included war, economic depression, and limited role choices in life, in addition to contraception that was uncertain at best.

The process and weight of making the "right" decisions are most extreme for well-educated young adults, who have the widest options but the greatest pressure to choose the best options—for education, career, lifestyle, and partner, even without adding a parenthood choice. As one 32-year-old said:

> I thought by now I would be more certain, more relaxed about where I've been, where I'm going, the choices I've made. But I'm not, and this parenthood choice just aggravates all those other gnawing doubts and fears about deciding that come out of the closet at night sometimes. Of course it's terribly important to make the right decision, but that doesn't help me decide; it just adds to the pressure.

This chapter has reviewed many of the reasons people give for delaying making a choice about parenthood. Some of the reasons have been described purposive, such completing educational or career goals; others are more contingent, such as developing a more stable relationship or feeling more settled. The more serious reasons for delay are those that involve profound discomfort; provision of further factual information can only partially address the emotional component involved in such delays. The next three chapters will address the major components in a parenthood decision, beginning with factual information and proceeding to more personal reactions and the uncertainties involved.

Notes

1. P. Daniels and K. Weingarten, *Sooner or Later: The Timing of Parenthood in Adult Lives* (New York: Norton, 1982).
2. This pattern of assuming parenthood "someday," but not for the present, was the most common characteristic of a group of couples who were still childless after age 30; many remained that way permanently. See J. Veevers, *Childless by Choice* (Toronto: Butterworth, 1980).
3. More extensive case histories of potential single parents facing these dilemmas and examples of two single women who successfully achieved parenthood under these circumstances are presented in M. Fabe and N. Wikler, *Up Against the Clock: Career Women Speak on the Choice to Have Children* (New York: Random House, 1979).
4. L. Eichenbaum and S. Orbach, *What Do Women Want: Exploding the Myth of Dependency* (New York: Coward-McCann, 1983); J.H. Scanzoni, *Sexual Bargaining: Power Politics in the American Marriage* (Englewood Cliffs, N.J.: Prentice-Hall, 1972); B.W. Brown, "Wife Employment and the Emergence of Egalitarian Marital Role Prescriptions," in G. Khurian and R. Ghosh (eds.), *Women in the Family and the Economy* (Westport, Conn.: Greenwood, 1981), pp. 231–243.
5. Fabe and Wikler, *Up Against the Clock.*
6. 1980 Roper National Opinion Poll, reported in L.C. Pogrebin, *Family Politics: Love and Power on an Intimate Frontier* (New York: McGraw-Hill, 1983).
7. A. Coleman and L. Coleman, *Earth Father/Sky Father: The Changing Concept of Fathering* (Englewood Cliffs, N.J.: Prentice-Hall, 1981). See also D. Coleman, "Sex Role Changes Baffle More Men," *New York Times,* August 27, 1984.
8. G. Steinem, "Words and Change," in *Outrageous Acts and Everyday Rebellions* (New York: Holt, Rinehart and Winston, 1983), pp. 149–160.
9. B. Rollin, "Motherhood: Who Needs It?" *Look,* September 22, 1970.

3
The Medical and Genetic Dimensions of the Parenthood Choice

Much of the literature on decisions about parenthood is focused on the pressure of the "biological clock," whose ticking indicates ever-increasing medical and genetic risks of pregnancy with advancing age. Many books on parenthood use this theme. Fabe and Wikler's *Up Against the Clock,* for example, reports interviews with career women who are trying to decide about parenthood after 30 and describes the experiences of some who have and have not chosen parenthood.[1] Their work will be used to illustrate many of the points made in these chapters. Rubin's book, which is more concerned with the genetic aspects of pregnancy after age 35, is reassuringly titled, *It's Not Too Late for a Baby.*[2]

Many people who feel pressured into making a decision about parenthood before they are ready report that their primary concern is not to wait too long—until pregnancy is not possible or until there are likely to be major problems for either child or mother. They assume that extra time equals extra risk—the longer you wait, the worse the odds are against you. Although there is some degree of truth in this assumption, the increased risk is small and far from universal at any age, and much new information from current research indicates that even this small risk can be reduced dramatically with current medical practices.

The first aspect of medical consideration is whether pregnancy will be possible if it is chosen. With the widespread availability of contraception, many people have not really tested their ability to conceive during the decade or more since they began sexual activity. Some of these people have discovered in their late twenties or thirties that the effort and expense of contraception may never have been necessary for them. Ironically, they may learn this only after extensive efforts to become parents, once they have made the decision to go ahead. Although there is some evidence that the likelihood of successful conception does decrease with age, the reasons for this are controversial, as is the available evidence on the issue.

This chapter will discuss the medical risks associated with parenthood, both those that increase with age and those that do not. It is important to present both categories, because many people assume that all medical risk increases with age, and they may be reassured to find that the vast majority of possible problems do not. Furthermore, many of the medical problems that have been associated with pregnancy at an older age are now manageable with newer high-risk care, which reduces the negative odds for these conditions to nearly normal. Most important, all of the medical conditions presented are rare in healthy women of any age; thus, the chances of successful pregnancy and delivery are excellent at any age.

Another concern for many potential parents has become acute recently with the increase in reports of environmental circumstances that can cause miscarriage or birth defects. The effects of drugs, infections, and other environmental factors that may be encountered (such as X rays) will also be discussed here.

Finally, there is the issue of increased risk of genetic defects in children born to older parents. A great deal of new information in this area has become available in the last decade. In general, this more recent news is reassuring to older potential parents, in that it has been found that most genetic conditions are extremely rare and that their risk does not increase with age at parenthood. Furthermore, with the increasing availability of parental diagnosis and genetic counseling, possible genetic problems often can be predicted before or early in pregnancy.

Increased Age and the Risk of Infertility

Many women who had delayed pregnancy to accomplish other goals were dismayed when the national media gave wide coverage to an editorial in the prestigious *New England Journal of Medicine,* which suggested that, for women, "the third decade should be devoted to childbearing and the fourth to career development."[3] "The spectre of infertility" with increased age left many readers with "a feeling of panic" or at least "urgency" and "diminished options . . . a sense of betrayal" when they were told that their deferral of pregnancy might well turn out to be permanent.[4]

Most researchers agree that increased age brings with it a reduction in the ability to become pregnant even when one intends to do so. The ability to conceive upon cessation of contraceptive efforts (and, of course, *with* efforts to conceive, through intercourse or artificial insemination) is technically termed *fecundability.* There is some indication that fecundability does decline with age, but almost everthing else about this issue is a subject of dispute.

One argument is that fecundability declines in direct association with increased age, from 20 on; however, this decline is argued to be due to the decline of frequency of intercourse over the same period. Clearly, the opportunity for conception cannot be more frequent than the opportunity for sperm and egg to meet under the proper circumstances. It is difficult to test this argument, because the only data on frequency of intercourse in large population samples do not provide information on biological capacity to conceive. Two indirect but clever kinds of information provide some clues on this issue. The first comes from a French study of women at infertility centers who had a normal ability to conceive but whose husbands had been found to be infertile.[5] These women were artificially inseminated at times coinciding with the most fertile days of their monthly cycles. The French researchers found that 74 percent of women under 30 conceived within twelve cycles, compared to 61 percent of women over 30. They thus concluded that there was a "slight but significant" decline in fecundability after age 30.

Another approach to this question of fecundability is provided by the research of Hendershot, using data from two national surveys of family growth from 1970 to 1975.[6] Women in this study were interviewed about both their planning and their actual experience of conception—whether conceptions that occurred were planned or unplanned and, if planned, what the duration of time was from "desired" to "achieved." Thus, *overdue conceptions* were defined as those that occurred later than planned or desired, indicating some limitation in the ability to conceive once conception was desired. If there is, in fact, a decline in fecundability with age, older mothers in the study should have reported a higher proportion of such overdue conceptions than their younger counterparts. Of the conceptions that occurred more than six months after they were desired, 12 percent were reported by mothers under age 25, compared to 23 percent among mothers aged 25 to 29 and 22 percent among mothers over 30. However, these older mothers were more likely than the younger ones to have to wait twelve months or more. Again, these data are for women who reported that they desired to have a child, but they do not include information on other factors, such as frequency of intercourse, that might affect the ability to conceive; nor do they include women who never succeeded in conceiving and delivering a live child.

The current state of knowledge on this issue may thus be summarized as necessarily incomplete. Probably the safest conclusion at present is that fecundability does decline somewhat with increased age but that it may be more a delay in conception than a permanent inability to conceive at all.

What Does "Increased Risk" Mean?

Throughout this book, you will frequently read that people who have a specific characteristic (such as high blood pressure, smoking more than a pack of cigarettes per day, or a history of pelvic inflammatory disease) are at *increased risk* with regard to a health or disease outcome, such as miscarriage or premature birth. This means that, in studies designed to assess such risk when all other factors in the study population are reasonably equal, people who have the risky behaviors or histories have been found to be more likely to experience the undesirable or unhealthy outcome than people who do not have those behaviors or histories.

In my profession, epidemiology (the term comes from the same Greek roots as *epidemic*), our research in the field of public health is designed to help us understand why some people in a given population stay well and others do not. This includes the study of epidemics, of course, but it also includes research on other aspects of health, such as pregnancy complications, diseases of genetic origin, and infant mortality. Unlike professionals in clinical medicine, who treat individual cases of illness, our work is to try to understand why some people are more or less likely to become ill in the first place.

Some of you may conclude from that last statement that epidemiologists study the cause of illness; if life were that simple, that is just what we would do. In a strict sense, however, few illnesses or health problems these days have a single, clear cause, if that means a single characteristic that, if present, always causes a specific illness. Even when we can identify a single agent, such as the tubercle bacillus that causes tuberculosis, we have to admit that although it is widespread in most environments, even today, few people come down with the disease. Therefore, we speak, instead, of a complex web of circumstances that may include an agent plus some relevant personal and environmental characteristics, all of which may be necessary before illness actually occurs. The presence of any one of these characteristics, or risk factors, increases the likelihood that illness may result, but it does not guarantee that it will occur in any single situation. In other words, we are talking about the odds of something occurring, in much the same way that racetrack odds makers, knowing something of the history of horse, jockey, weather, and track conditions, will give you 15 to 1 on horse A but only 3 to 1 on horse B.

Unlike horseracing, however, our statements of relative risk derive from research based on scientific rules about population size, representativeness, and procedures to be followed. If you are to be a discerning judge of many of the "health" claims presented to you in daily life, you must consider them in the same way. Statements about increased risk should lead you to assess, at least, how much risk? . . . to whom? . . . and under what circumstances?

If you read, for example, that people with green eyes are three times as likely to have a severe reaction to drug A, and you have green eyes, you may be worried. Suppose, however, that you read further and find that this conclusion is based on a study that reported 6 cases of severe reaction among 6,000 green-eyed people who took the drug during the period of study. Thus, your relative risk may be greater, but your absolute risk is still only 1 in 1,000.

An additional example concerns the more complex issue of risk circumstances. If we ask about the effect of drinking alcoholic beverages on pregnancy loss (miscarriage), there are studies that have found that women who drink before and during early pregnancy have a higher risk of miscarriage, but there are also studies that report that there is no increased risk for drinkers compared to nondrinkers.[7] Here is a situation in which circumstances other than drinking may not always be equal. If there are more smokers among the drinking group than among the nondrinkers, we would expect more miscarriages among the drinking group, because smokers are more likely to have miscarriages, among other pregnancy problems. However, if the studies that found no increased miscarriage risk had chosen groups in which that smoking and other risky characteristics were more balanced between the groups, they might well have found no risk or less risk due to drinking per se. Life and health are complicated issues. Sometimes, even with the best available efforts, all we can say is that we have some reason to be concerned about increased risk, but we cannot be sure.

Finally, remember, also, that statements of risk are about groups, not about individuals. Your risk as a member of a group may be 1 in 10 or 1 in 1,000, but nothing guarantees that you will or will not be that one. Only you can judge which risks and odds you can live with.

Increased Age and Medical Risk

The first important point in discussing both medical and genetic risk is to emphasize that there is no threshold of age beyond which the dangers to parent or child increase dramatically. Indeed, most conditions of risk exist at any age; that is, they do not continue to increase as one gets older. By and large, most medical conditions that increase risk are associated with poor physical condition or lack of proper medical surveillance, both of which are correctible at any age. Much current information indicates that women and men today are in better physical condition during their active adult years than those in past parenthood generations, as a result of better nutrition, more exercise, and generally better health habits, such as less smoking, moderate alcohol use, and the like.[8] To the extent that these changes have occurred, the statistics of the past that indicated increased risk for older mothers are not valid predictors of what will happen in the same age group today or tomorrow, because they were based on a cohort of women in worse physical condition and with less medical knowledge and treatment for problems of pregnancy and delivery. Much of the excess morbidity and mortality reported in earlier vital statistics was based on women who were poor, who already had large families, and who had poor nutrition and little rest or prenatal care—women very different from those who are considering parenthood at an older age today. Such women were also more likely to have conditions such as diabetes, hypertension, and reproductive system problems from earlier pregnancies, all of which increase pregnancy risk when they are not cared for prenatally.

Early Pregnancy Loss

The most common risk of pregnancy is that it will terminate early. Although it is impossible to find completely accurate statistics, because some pregnancies end even before they are recognized as pregnancies, most estimates are that from 15 to 25 percent of all pregnancies terminate in spontaneous abortion, usually during the first three months.[9] Furthermore, the likelihood of early pregnancy loss is increased if there is a history of prior miscarriage. From this observation alone, it should be clear that older parents also have more risk of miscarriage, because they have longer reproductive histories than younger people.

Since many pregnancies that terminate very early may not even be recognized as pregnancies, the precise risk of early pregnancy termination cannot be known for women of any age. However, for those in whom spontaneous abortion is diagnosed, the most common cause is abnormal development of the fetus itself, rather than circumstances in the pregnancy environment, such as the condition of the mother. More than half of all spontaneous abortions are due to chromosomal abnormalities, and such abnormalities occur regardless of the age of either parent.[10] Another common cause is such developmental abnormalities as spina bifida, major cardiovascular abnormalities, and other conditions that would be lethal in any case. These developmental abnormalities are of complex origin; their precise cause is often unknown, although several environmental causes, such as viral infections and exposure to dangerous agents, have been associated with increased risk.[11]

Women who have persistent problems with early miscarriage can often be helped by correction of gynecological problems or other medical problems. For those with no identified physical problem, psychotherapy has been reported to help a significant proportion of treated women achieve full-term pregnancy, either by helping them resolve their ambivalence and anxiety about pregnancy or by a more general approach to stress and tension management through relaxation and other techniques.

One type of early pregnancy loss that has caused concern because of its apparent increase during the last decade is ectopic pregnancy, in which the implantation of a fertilized egg occurs outside its normal location in the uterus, usually in one of the fallopian tubes. As in a normal pregnancy, the egg continues to grow and establish a placenta, but eventually, at about five to eight weeks after conception, the tube can rupture, spilling its contents and blood into the abdominal cavity and causing serious, even life-threatening complications. Although doctors have become more adept at recognizing ectopic pregnancies (many used to be diagnosed as appendicitis), there is no doubt that an alarming increase has occurred in the rate of such pregnancies. Three studies in this country—in New York, Washington, and nationwide—as well as reports from other countries, such as Britain and Sweden, have confirmed significant increases in this problem during the last decade.[12] Although the cause of many ectopic pregnancies is unknown, several factors have been identified as leading to increased risk. The most important of these factors is the increase in conditions leading to damage of the fallopian tubes themselves, so that a fertilized egg has more difficulty moving along the tube toward the uterus. For example, cases of pelvic inflammatory disease (PID) have increased during this period, and a major effect of PID is scarring and blockage of the fallopian tubes. Even if PID is treated with antibiotics, therapy may begin too late to prevent some scarring. Another group at increased risk are the so-called DES daughters—women whose mothers took the drug diethylstilbestrol during their pregnancies in the 1950s and 1960s; these women have been found to have a variety of reproductive tract problems, including malformed tubes. Some contraceptives, especially the intrauterine device (IUD), also increase risk. Of course, the longer a woman has been sexually active and used contraception, the more chance there has been for these conditions to have occurred, so older women have been found to have higher rates of ectopic pregnancy.[13]

Fibroids and Endometriosis

Two other problems of the female reproductive system that increase with age may cause complications when fertility and pregnancy are desired: fibroid tumors (known as *fibroids*)and endometriosis. Fibroids—benign growths of the uterus that range in size from very small to larger than a grapefruit may occur in more than one-third of all women by age 40. In endometriosis, which is less common but more difficult to diagnose, cells from the endometrium, the lining of the uterus, migrate outside that organ and may attach themselves anywhere within the pelvic cavity—on ovaries, fallopian tubes, or other areas—where they can block fertilization or proper implantation of a fertilized egg. Little is known about the causes or extent of this problem, but it seems to occur more often in career women who work under high stress and who have deferred parenthood.[14] A history of either of these conditions indicates that more than the usual problems may occur when pregnancy is planned or attempted.

If you are concerned because of your medical history regarding any of the conditions mentioned here (fibroids, endometriosis, PID, previous spontaneous abortion), you may wish to consult a specialist in fertility even before planning parenthood. Large medical centers and teaching hospitals often have fertility clinics; you can also obtain names of qualified specialists from the Planned Parenthood office in your area or from the American Fertility Society (see the resources section at the end of this book).

Health Habits and Medical Problems of Pregnancy

Health habits also affect pregnancy risk. Alcohol consumption, for example, is associated with many kinds of problems for the pregnancy and the fetus. In one study, miscarriage rates for women who drink have been found to be over twice as high as those for nondrinkers. Furthermore, there is much higher risk of birth defects and mental retardation among offspring of women who drink frequently.[15]

Similarly, smoking has been found to double the risk of spontaneous abortion, and it has been reported that smoking by either parent increases the likelihood of delivery complications and low birth weight in pregnancies that do proceed to term.[16]

The Effects of Chronic Conditions on Pregnancy

Some medical problems of pregnancy are associated with chronic conditions that become more frequent with aging in any population, such as hypertension, diabetes, vascular and kidney diseases, and abnormalities of the reproductive system. Any of these conditions can occur at any age, but they are more likely to be found among 40-year olds than among 20-year-olds. Three important points must be noted regarding these conditions, however. First, such conditions are relatively rare, even among those in their forties, and they are even more unlikely to be found among people with health lifestyles, as described earlier. Second, people with such conditions can and do succeed in becoming parents, although they must expect to work more closely with medical professionals involved in pregnancy and delivery. Third, an entire area of specialization in such high-risk pregnancy has been developed, and there are now many facilities in which the risk to both parents and child can be reduced to nearly normal.

The basic principles in dealing with these conditions are similar. Each condition has the effect of making it more difficult for the mother to meet the increased physiological demands of a pregnancy or of compromising the efficiency with which the growing fetus is able to obtain the necessary nutrients and other environmental conditions necessary for normal growth. Therefore, careful medical monitoring is necessary to help the ongoing processes of adjustment to the developing pregnancy and delivery.

Successful pregnancy and delivery are increasingly possible for women with any of these conditions, but they must be willing to understand the problem and work closely with the professionals involved in achieving a common goal. This close cooperation should start before pregnancy, when potential parents are considering whether or not to go ahead with parenthood. Preliminary planning and diagnosis are essential for several reasons. First, it is very valuable to have baseline measurements so that the changes that may occur as pregnancy progresses can be monitored. Of considerable importance, too, is that many of the most commonly used drugs for these conditions have been implicated, if not established, as contributors to increased risk of birth defects. Their potential adverse effects are most severe early in pregnancy, when major development of fetal organ and limb systems are taking place. Potential damage during early—perhaps unrecognized—pregnancy can be avoided if medication changes are arranged before beginning a pregnancy.

Assuming that such cooperative assessment and planning do take place, the increased risk to parent or child during pregnancy, even when the mother has a chronic medical condition, is generally quite low. Table 3–1 summarizes the most common medical conditions and their potential effects on pregnancy.

Even among potential parents who are insulin-dependent diabetics, morbidity and mortality rates for both mother and child have decreased dramatically during the last decade. This decrease is due, in part, to more meticulous monitoring and management of maternal glucose levels throughout the pregnancy and, in part, to newer techniques for assessing the condition of the fetus during its development, especially during the last two months of gestation. Careful management can prolong even the most difficult pregnancies until the fetus is mature enough to do well even with early delivery. Several studies in medical units that have used both advances report fetal death rates no higher than in the nondiabetic population, prenatal mortality rates less than 5 percent, and a major birth malformation rate of less than 9 percent, compared to approximately 2 percent in nondiabetic populations.[17] At present, efforts are under way to reduce the risk of major birth malformation by more careful monitoring and management of insulin-dependent diabetes during the first trimester of pregnancy, when such major developmental defects would occur. One recent study reported a lower incidence of major birth defects among women who attended a special diabetes clinic before becoming pregnant, presumably because these women had more normal glucose levels at conception and during the crucial early weeks of pregnancy.[18]

Basically, anyone over 35 who is considering parenthood should first have a thorough physical examination, including a discussion of health habits and nutrition patterns. This would be wise for both male and female poten-

Table 3–1
Some Medical Conditions Associated with Increased Age and Their Potential Effects on Pregnancy

Condition	Possible Effects
Uterine fibroids or myomas—benign tumors of the uterus—existing prior to pregnancy (20 percent of women over 35)	Hormones associated with pregnancy can increase tumor growth. May be confused with multiple birth. Can obstruct vaginal delivery if located near cervix. Complication rate is generally low.
Hypertension—sustained high blood pressure—existing prior to pregnancy	Medications may affect pregnancy or fetus; with careful monitoring, risk is low. Can lead to eclampsia (convulsions), a serious risk during first pregnancy if associated with edema and proteinuria.
Gestational hypertension (toxemia), occurring only during pregnancy	Increased blood pressure, greater demand on kidney and cardiovascular system. May require early inducement of labor or cesarean section.
Adult-onset diabetes Diagnosed prior to pregnancy	If diet-controlled, no added risk to mother, small added risk to child. If insulin-dependent, varies widely, needs careful monitoring; little added risk to mother; fetal risk increases with duration of the disease, but complication risk is less than 10 percent.
Diagnosed during pregnancy	Mild symptoms can be controlled with diet; more severe symptoms may require insulin. Some increased risk to mother and fetus, especially stillbirth.

tial parents, since there is evidence that the health status of the father also affects the likelihood of achieving successful pregnancy and delivery as well as making a social and genetic contribution to parenthood. Such examinations and discussions with professionals who are oriented toward preventive medicine can reduce the medical risks of pregnancy and anxiety about it and can encourage the maintenance of health habits that are beneficial whether or not parenthood is the outcome.

Increased Likelihood of Multiple Births

Of the complications of pregnancy that are more common among older parents, only one has been found to occur regardless of health condition and the extent of prenatal care. This "complication" is the increased likelihood of twins and, much more rarely, of triplets or more. Chances of multiple births are less than one in a hundred for mothers under age 30, but this likelihood increases to one in approximately seventy-five between ages 30 and 35 and one in sixty-five between ages 35 and 40; it then decreases after age 40 to approximately the same odds as for younger mothers.[19]

The majority of twins are fraternal (nonidentical, or dizygotic); they account for approximately three out of every four twin births. A history of twins in either family increases the likelihood of twin birth in all family members, not just in twins themselves; and this likelihood does not skip generations, as folklore indicates. Dizygotic twins are separate but simultaneous fertilizations of two eggs by two sperm and therefore can vary as much as any two siblings born to the same parents. They can be of different sexes, and have different hair and eye colors, different size, different temperaments, and so forth. The frequency of dizogytic twin births increases with maternal age.

The frequency of identical (monozygotic) twin births does not increase with increased maternal age. Monozygotic twins are the result of fertilization of a single egg by a single sperm, but a division of the cell mass into two identical parts occurs early in the development of the fetus. Such twins are therefore genetically identical, although environmental differences before or after birth can make them appear to be different.

Some older parents feel that the risk of multiple births is beneficial in one respect. Although twins are more difficult to deal with both before and after birth—just in terms of the resources required to meet their needs—the fact that most of these twins are fraternal (dizygotic) rather than identical (monozygotic) means that many later-starting parents are able to achieve an instant ideal family size for them, with a good chance of one boy and one girl.

The increased number of multiple births to older parents is another example of how information on risk in this age group is changing. Previously, since the likelihood of twins increased both with the age of the mother and the number of previous pregnancies, the multiple births that did occur were more likely to have complications. Also, since multiple births often do not go to full term, the prematurity of many of these infants also contributed to poor outcomes. With current health practices and standards of care, however, most twin pregnancies now occur in mothers who are in better physical condition. Even in pregnancies that end prematurely, infant survival rates exceed 90 percent, a far cry from the survival rates of less than 50 percent a generation ago.[20]

Other Pregnancy Complications

There are several other complications of pregnancy for which older mothers are at slightly increased risk. Each of these conditions is rare but does occur more frequently among older mothers, especially among those with the other conditions already discussed, such as hypertension or diabetes, and among those who smoke. Each of these can still result in a successful pregnancy and delivery can result even with these complications, although more careful monitoring may be necessary during the pregnancy, and intervention for delivery, such as cesarean section, may be needed.

One complication that occurs in approximately 1 in every 200 advanced pregnancies is placenta praevia, in which the placenta (the tissue that connects the maternal and fetal circulations, thereby providing nutrients to the fetus) is attached to the uterine wall low enough to be near or even over the cervix.[21] This location provides poor support, and the placenta becomes increasingly vulnerable to damage as the pregnancy progresses. This condition can cause bleeding severe enough to endanger both mother and child, and it may require early delivery by cesarean section. In some cases, however, the placenta starts off low in the uterus but later moves up the wall of the uterus to a more normal position and causes no problems.

Another complication, intrauterine growth retardation, occurs when the placenta does not supply enough nourishment to the fetus to permit a normal rate of growth and development. This condition is more likely in the presence of any of the already mentioned conditions that limit the ability of the mother to adapt to the additional demands of pregnancy—for example, hypertension, diabetes, heart disease, or placenta praevia. Unfortunately, some women still believe that minimal weight gain during pregnancy is desirable, and they eat an insufficient amount to nourish normal fetal growth, especially in the later months. Children born under such conditions are designated small for gestational age (SGA); in addition to reduced size, they have less body fat and are therefore less resistant to cold and more susceptible to hypoglycemia (low blood sugar).[22]

Finally, there is some increased tendency for older mothers to have prolonged or difficult labor. Some experts report that prolonged labor is less likely to occur among older mothers who are in good physical condition, noting that it is more likely only if the mother is obese or has poor muscle tone or other physical complications, such as large fibroids of the uterus.[23] The increased risk of perinatal loss due to prolonged or difficult labor has been virtually eliminated, however, by good obstetric care, since careful monitoring and prompt intervention can provide alternatives that have less risk of complications to either mother or child.

In summary, current medical and research information indicates that most of the problems associated with increased risk of pregnancy from a medical standpoint have been solved and are rare in healthy women of any age. For the problems that do persist, current methods of high-risk pregnancy care can reduce the risks associated with such complications to near normal in most cases.

Environmental Risks

One concern expressed by many potential parents is that, in the course of their adult lives, they might have been exposed to (or might have exposed themselves to) factors in their environment that could prevent pregnancy, have negative consequences on the pregnancy, or increase their risk of giving birth to a child with physical or mental abnormalities. Such harmful factors are called *teratogens,* which means that they have destructive effects on normal fetal development. Some of these teratogens, such as X-ray exposure and exposure to certain chemicals, can be harmful both before and during pregnancy, whereas others are dangerous only during the first three months of gestation, the most crucial period in the development of the fetus. Potential parents should be aware that some environmental exposures to either the father or the mother can have teratogenic effects. Recent research has indicated that many occupational exposures to men have affected their subsequent fertility and have increased the risk of birth defects in their children.

Unfortunately, the longer people wait to make a decision about parenthood, the longer they have to become exposed to potentially harmful environmental situations. Our knowledge about environmental risks is increasing rapidly, but much of the information now available is incomplete and controversial. For every documented occupational exposure risk, there are dozens more that are currently suspect but cannot be investigated properly because of lack of funds or qualified personnel. At present, experts agree that many substances that are part of our lives are suspect, but few are proven dangers.[24] Recent summaries of some environmental risks are provided in tables 3–2 and 3–3, which list established and suspect occupational exposures, drugs, and infections. We are not yet able to be specific for many other environmental categories.

For most people in most occupations, there is little additional risk with added years of work. Even for people who are employed in higher-risk occupations, more stringent safety regulations now exist for many occupational settings that expose workers to radioactivity, anesthetic gases, lead, vinyl chloride, and similar substances. However, enforcement of safety standards is far from uniform, even for such known hazards, and many companies evade the issue by not hiring women of childbearing age or by requiring waivers or proof of sterility. We cannot be proud of the present record of the United States in protecting the safety and future health of its workers and their families. One force for improvement in this area must be better informed and more politically active employees, working with health professionals to monitor and publicize potentially harmful situations in their environment. Since environments that increase the risk of pregnancy loss and birth defects usually also contribute to increased risk of development of many types of cancer later in life, improvement in such conditions on the basis of

Table 3–2
Environmental/Occupational Exposures Suspected of Causing Damage to Fetal Growth or Development

Anesthetic gases	Methyl mercury
Cadmium	Monosodium glutamate (MSG)
Cyclamates	Nitrates
DDT and metabolites	Nitrites
Dioxin (TCDD)	Organic Solvents
Food colorings	Polyhalogenated biphenyls
Hair dyes and sprays	Radiation
Herbicides	Saccharin
Hydrocarbons	Smelter gases
Lead	2,4,5-T (agent orange)

Source: Compiled from data in R. Brent and M. Harris (eds.), *Prevention of Embryonic, Fetal, and Perinatal Disease,* DHEW Pub. No. (NIH)76–853 (Bethesda, Md.: National Institutes of Health, 1976); and H. Kalter and J. Warkany, "Congenital Malformations: Etiologic Factors and Their Role in Prevention." *New England Journal of Medicine* 308 (1983):424–431, 491–497.

Table 3–3
Drugs and Infections That Can Damage Fetal Growth or Development

Drugs known to be damaging
   Alcohol
   Androgens (male hormones)
   Anticancer drugs
   Antiseizure drugs (phenytoin, trimethadione)
   Anticlotting drugs (coumadin, warfarin)
   Estrogen (DES)
   Heroin
   Methadone
   Nicotine
   Thalidomide

Drugs that are suspect at this time
   Antibiotics (e.g., chloramphenicol, streptomycin, tetracycline)
   Antinauseants (Bendectin, Debendox)
   Cafergot
   Diuretics (hydrochlorothiazide)
   Hexachlorophene
   Lithium
   LSD
   Marijuana
   Oral drugs for diabetes (Tolbutamide)
   Progestins
   Sulfa drugs
   Thiouracil
   Tranquilizers (diazepam, meprobamate, chlordiazepoxide)

Table 3–3 continued

Infections that can be damaging
  Chicken pox
  Coxsackie B virus
  Cytomegalovirus (CMV)
  Hepatitis
  Herpes simplex
  Influenza
  Rubella (German measles)
  Smallpox (now eliminated, but see below)
  Syphillis
  Toxoplasmosis
  Vaccinia (for smallpox vaccination)
  Various types of equine encephalitis (Venezuelan, St. Louis)

---

reproductive "early warning" information may well reduce cancer risk for all who are exposed as they grow older.

One essential preventive measure for prospective parents is to be sure that they are immune to measles (rubella). They can be certain by obtaining a vaccination or by having a blood test that provides evidence that they are already immune. Some people may think that exposure to measles in early pregnancy, with the attendant risk of severe birth defects from congenital rubella syndrome, is an issue of the past; unfortunately, however, recent health information indicates that the problem is far from eliminated in this country. In 1982, the most recent year for which statistics are available, serious outbreaks of measles occurred in young adults, among hospital personnel particularly, with more than a thousand cases among persons over 20 years of age.[25] Unfortunately, among these adults were some pregnant women, and an estimated 90 children were born with congenital rubella syndrome. The Centers for Disease Control estimate that as many as 20 percent of all women at risk have not been immunized against measles, because they completed their primary education before the current requirement for immunization at school entry went into effect. They recommend a strong effort to immunize all women of childbearing age. This effort would include making immunization part of routine visits to gynecologists, obstetricians, or family planning clinics; making it a requirement for obtaining a marriage license; and requiring proof of immunity for college entrance or for employment in occupations that have contact with pregnant women.

Risks Associated with Delivery

There is alwasy some potential risk for both mother and infant in the process of delivery, regardless of the age of the mother. It is also true, however, that medical advances have markedly reduced these risks during the last decade. As the birth rate has declined, fewer hospitals provide obstetric services; the net result has been that most of the older, smaller units have been phased out, and more specialized alternative facilities, providing more extensive services and staffed by better trained personnel, have been developed. As in many areas of medical care, obstetric systems of graduated levels of care have evolved, and women with potential pregnancy problems can be referred to specialized facilities.

Some obstetricians consider any pregnancy of a woman over 35 to be of potentially higher risk; they may do so, however, on the basis of the statistics discussed earlier as being generally out of date. Other obstetricians take a broader view, balancing the health and condition of the parents against the importance of the situation. More than one specialist has expressed the opinion that any pregnancy at this age is "special," in that there may not be another chance, and therefore has advocated special care to ensure the best possible outcome for the infant—even if this means a greater likelihood of artificial intervention, including cesarean section.

It should not be surprising, then to discover that the chances of delivering a child by cesarean section are greater for older mothers. Of the deliveries in community hospitals in this country in 1981, for example, 18 percent were by cesarean section, but the proportion was 24 percent for mothers over age 35 and 32 percent for mothers in that age group who were delivering their first child.[26] Table 3–4 shows data on cesarean section deliveries in this country since 1965. They have increased fourfold during that time, but it is clear that this dramatic increase is not entirely due to the increased proportion of older parents having a first child. The rate of cesarean section deliveries has increased for all age groups, and it has actually increased more gradually for the older age groups than for the population as a whole. A great deal of concern has been expressed about whether all these surgical deliveries are really necessary, especially since rates in this country far exceed those reported for other countries where statistics on problems at delivery and infant mortality are as good or better than ours. The additional information that cesarean sections are much more frequent in private hospitals and among patients covered by health and hospital insurance suggests that at least some of them are not really necessary.

In addition to the two types of obstetricians already described, there is a growing group of physicians who are delighted with their more mature parents. They have recognized that these potential parents are the most educated and motivated of any age group. They have found that such parents-to-be ask a lot of questions, take the proper precautions, and are active participants in pursuing the common goal of helping the pregnancy go as well as possible. These obstetricians do not mean that such patients are anxious, worried, or demanding people in comparison to younger patients.

Table 3–4
Cesarean Section Rates for Births in Community Hospitals, 1965–1981

	Percentage of All Births, by Mother's Age		
Year	*All Ages*	*30–34*	*Over 35*
1981	17.9	21.3	24.4
1980	16.5	18.0	20.6
1975	10.4	13.6	15.0
1970	5.5	7.5	8.3
1965	4.5	6.4	7.9

Source: P. Placek, S. Taffel, and M. Moien, "Cesarean Section Delivery Rates: United States, 1981," *American Journal of Public Health* 73(1983):861–862.

Note: The highest rates are for primiparas, in the northeast United States, in larger hospitals, especially proprietary ones, and when covered by Blue Cross and other insurance.

On the contrary, they describe older parents-to-be as being delighted about the pregnancy, less conflicted about it, and more prepared, in a positive sense, for the changes that occur. As one physician states:

> They have put a great deal of thought into this pregnancy, as they have put a great deal of thought into what they have already done . . . they have measured their careers and have made a judgment somewhere along the line that now is the right time to have a child. Having done this, they are completely ready to devote themselves to this particular challenge. They take it with a great deal of enthusiasm and do really well. They are much more informed . . . and find the pregnancy . . . more satisfying.[27]

There is ample research evidence to indicate that people who face a stressful situation with a sense that they have made the right decision, and who feel that they have the right resources to deal with the situation, do in fact cope with it better.

More obstetricians who deliver patients of all ages now feel that physical condition is much more important than chronological age in anticipating problems connected with delivery. Clearly, a woman of 25 who is in poor physical condition, who has not received proper nutrition or prenatal care, or who has continued to practice poor health habits, such as smoking and drinking, is at much higher risk of delivery complications, for both herself and the baby, than a woman of 40 who has none of these risk-predicting characteristics. All other things being equal, women of any age who are in good health are likely to have successful deliveries.

There are slightly increased chances of several kinds of complications for older women, but they can generally be described as limited to situations in which the potential for increased risk was already known. These possible complications—low birth weight, perinatal loss (stillbirth at any time after twenty-eight weeks of pregnancy or death during the period just after birth), the need for cesarean section delivery—happen more often to older women because proportionately more older mothers have twins (who often arrive early and thus have lower birth weights than single births) or have other conditions associated with aging, such as hypertension or diabetes.

Most older parents, however, have successful deliveries and healthy, normal infants. Although there are many descriptions of the experience by ecstatic new parents, few systematic descriptions have appeared of the current cohort of older parents. One study begun in 1981 by Dr. Iris Kern in Washington, D.C., involved seventy-five mothers between the ages of 38 and 49 who had eighty-three babies among them.[28] Of these women, 80 percent reported that they delivered their babies normally (vaginally), and nearly three-fourths of these did so without needing any medication to reduce pain. When we consider that the national average for cesarean section in this age group is now nearly one-fifth of all births, the experience of this older group is quite positive. Kern reports that the vast majority of women she interviewed claimed that the experience of pregnancy was more positive than they had dared to imagine.

There are many alternatives to the hospital-based, medication-assisted birth today. Although many obstetricians advise against these alternatives for older parents, some physicians and their patients have considered it safe for parents over 35 or even 40 to consider alternative birth arrangements if the mother is healthy and if the delivery is expected to be normal. Most insist, however, that backup specialized facilities be available close by, just in case. Since children born to parents who use any of the variety of prior conditioning and training methods to avoid the need for medication or artificial intervention generally do better at and after birth, these options should be available to parents of all ages.

The Potential for Birth Defects in Children Born to Older Parents

Birth defects include any malformations of physical or mental structure or function that are present at birth. Some, of course, are much more serious than others. Birth defects are conventionally categorized as minor defects, such as extra fingers or toes, and major ones, such as hemophilia (an inherited absence of the blood-clotting factor) or major defects of any organ system, such as the heart.

Congenital Defects

Some birth defects are congenital; that is, the child is born with them but did not inherit them from its parents. Congenital defects are caused by external influences that occur before or during the pregnancy, including drugs, such as Thalidomide, which interfered with the development of cells that formed arms and legs; viruses, such as rubella (measles), which can cause a cluster of defects known as the congenital rubella syndrome, affecting the heart, vision, hearing, and mental development; and other environmental exposures discussed earlier, such as radiation. The most severe congenital defects occur because of the mother's exposure to the harmful influences during the first fifty-five days of pregnancy, when major cell differentiation is occurring and major organ systems are developing in the fetus.

Other congenital defects can be caused by external influences that occur after fifty-five days of fetal development, up to and including the birth process. Generally, such harmful influences influence the ability of the fetus to develop normally and grow at the proper rate. Thus, maternal conditions that interfere with the blood supply to the growing fetus—such as smoking, high blood pressure, diabetes, or kidney disease—may cause lack of brain development, or even brain damage, by impairing the supply of oxygen to the baby's brain. These later circumstances, including complications that occur during delivery, are considered congenital, because they are not inherited from parents or grandparents. Thus, in discussing the relative risk of such harmful influences in children born to older mothers, we need to consider how, and in what ways, the environment and health habits of parents may differ by age. Also, we must obtain information on the relative likelihood of potential parents having various chronic diseases associated with increased age, such as high blood pressure and diabetes, and learn how these diseases affect the risk of birth defects.

Genetic Defects

The other major type of birth defects is those caused by abnormalities in the genetic background of the parents. These defects are both congenital (the child is born with them) and inherited, meaning that they come not from the environment but from the chromosomes passed to the child by each parent. Most genetic defects occur rarely, but knowledge about them has increased dramatically during the last twenty years with developments in the field of genetics and with the prenatal genetic counseling that is now available in most medical centers.

Risk from Genetic Abnormalities

Older people who are considering parenthood are most concerned about the possibility that they may give birth to a child with severe birth defects caused by some genetic abnormality. Most of them have heard of or know someone with a child who has mongolism, or Down syndrome—a genetic abnormality that results in specific physical abnormalities and, usually, profound mental retardation—and they also have heard that the risk of having such a child increases with age.

All human cells have forty-six chromosomes; when an egg from the mother and a sperm cell from the father unite, each contributes twenty-three chromosomes to determine the characteristics of the new life. When chromosomal errors occur, they are of two kinds: an excess of chromosomes (for example, forty-seven instead of forty-six) or chromosomal "breakage," in which there is the correct number of chromosomes but their internal arrangement is disrupted. Down syndrome, for example, is also called trisomy 21, because fetuses with this syndrome have three of chromosome number 21, instead of the normal two. It is the most common of the major chromosomal abnormalities with which the fetus is likely to survive. Although there are many reasons why chromosomal abnormalities occur, most of the severe ones are not compatible with survival; pregnancies that occur with such abnormalities are most likely to terminate as early spontaneous abortions.

The serious defects caused by chromosomal disturbance or dislocation are generally classified into two types: inborn errors of biochemical processing and hereditary diseases that are sex-linked, such as hemophilia. Most of the former defects involve hereditary deficiencies in some enzyme activity in the body, so that a person born with the condition may be unable to process carbohydrates, lipids, or certain proteins normally. Others involve abnormal storage of substances, such as certain minerals, to the point that they become toxic. There are more than a hundred such inherited conditions, most of which can now be diagnosed through amniocentesis and other genetic screening. What is important, however, is that most of these defects are quite rare, and none except the Down syndrome type show any increased risk with increased maternal or paternal age.

Since Down syndrome is the most common severe birth defect risk associated with increased age, a great deal of information is available on the relative risk of having a child with the condition. These statistics are usually provided by age group; for example, one can read that the risk of having an affected child for mothers aged 30 to 35 years old is approximately one in every 840 live births. Since the risk increases gradually with each increased year of age, however, such statistics are not very helpful for individual decision making. Furthermore, some research evidence indicates that the risk is also related to the age of the father; in at least one study, twenty-four Down syndrome births were traced to chromosomal abnormality in the father instead of the mother. If this pattern is found in other studies, most current information about the risk of having a child with this syndrome will have to be revised to take into account the age of *both* parents.

Only one large study has estimated the risk of Down syndrome according to maternal age by year.[29] The data, based on a large cohort of births in

Table 3-5
Estimated Rates of Down Syndrome in Live Births
(New York State)

Mother's Age	Risk/Births
30	1/885
31	1/826
32	1/725
33	1/592
34	1/465
35	1/365
36	1/287
37	1/225
38	1/177
39	1/139
40	1/109
41	1/85
42	1/67
43	1/53
44	1/41
45	1/32

Source: E.B. Hook and E.M. Chambers, "Estimated Rates of Down Syndrome in Live Births by One Year Maternal Age Intervals for Mothers Aged 20–49 in a New York State Study," in D. Bergsma and B.R. Lowry (eds.), *Numerical Taxonomy and Polygenic Disorders* (New York: National Foundation—March of Dimes, 1977), pp. 123–141.

upstate New York, indicate the risk by mother's age at delivery (see table 3–5). These statistics were gathered prior to the availability of amniocentesis, however; therefore, they represent rates that are no longer seen, since many parents who learn that a particular pregnancy has this unfortunate characteristic choose to terminate it by abortion. (See the next section of this chapter for a detailed discussion of amniocentesis and other prenatal testing procedures.) It is also true, however, that even without further knowledge, the chances that a 35-year-old mother will have a child with Down syndrome are now less than one in 350; for a 40-year-old mother, the chances are still less than one in 100 for any given pregnancy.

Amniocentesis is an expensive procedure, but increasing numbers of older parents are choosing to have it done because it can provide information on the major single cause of concern about having a child in later years. The availability of the procedure is becoming more widespread, and the costs are increasingly covered by medical insurance plans. In many areas, funding for the testing can be provided by the local birth defects foundation upon recommendation by the physician that the patient is at increased risk because of age or family history of genetic disorders.

For many people, the availability of advance information on this kind of risk provides the reassurance they feel they need to consider pregnancy at this point in their lives. They have an amniocentesis done because they want to be reassured that there are no major abnormalities in chromosomes or fetal development. Such procedures are used, however, to detect abnormality because there is some increased risk; they do not guarantee that everything will be normal. That is why the testing should be accompanied by counseling; if the news from the testing is not good, parents should have all the information they need to consider their options from that point forward. Most parents whose results are negative choose abortion, but there are conditions that can be treated, even prior to delivery, allowing nearly normal lives for those who are born with them.

A study of 2,200 married women members of a Blue Cross plan in 1981 indicated that among women aged 35 to 45 who had not already permanently achieved sterilization and were undecided about whether to have any or more children, 73 percent of those aged 35 to 39 and 87 percent of those aged 40 to 45 reported that the reassurance provided by amniocentesis would increase their willingness to consider having children.[30] There is ample evidence that parents are very concerned about the potential health and quality of life of their children, and they may be willing to sacrifice quantity to achieve better quality in this respect. In this same study, 62 percent of those who found out that their unborn child had major defects chose abortion. The authors add that their clinical experience was that an even greater proportion of parents made the choice to terminate a pregnancy with major defects when the situation was not hypothetical but real. In another study, involving the results of 2,404 amniocenteses performed on women over 35 at one medical center from 1970 to 1978 (see table 3–6), 94 percent of the women whose test results indicated the presence of chromosomal abnormalities chose to terminate their pregnancies.[31]

Table 3–6
Results of 2,404 Amniocenteses Performed on Women over 35 at One Medical Center from 1970 to 1978

Age Range	Number of Women	Findings	
		Normal	*Abnormal*
40 +	561	534 (95.2%)	27 (4.8%)
35–39	1,843	1,817 (98.6%)	26 (1.4%)

Source: Data compiled from the experience of the University of California Medical Center, and consistent with the results from other major U.S. and Canadian Studies. See National Institute of Child Health and Human Development, *Antenatal Diagnosis: Report of a Consensus Development Conference,* p. I–66.

Prenatal Testing for Birth Defects

A resource for potential parents that has grown rapidly in the last decade is the availability of testing before and during pregnancy for the possibility of birth defects, along with counseling services to explain and advise about the test results and the alternatives available for those whose findings are causes for concern. Since much of the information used in such counseling is based on the study of genetics, this service is often called genetic counseling, but it can include advice about some birth defects that are not necessarily genetic in origin.

Such testing and counseling is done by physicians who specialize in genetic diseases and by genetic counselors who have received graduate training in both genetics and counseling. These services should be used by people who are concerned, because of their age or family history, about the possibility of having a child with an inherited disease or defect. Thorough testing and counseling procedures include, first, compilation of detailed information about the health of the parents and their relatives. Various tests can also be performed to determine whether the potential parents or other family members are carriers of certain diseases. For many diseases, information can be provided about the relative risk of the disease in pregnancy, the severity of the disease, whether treatment is available, and whether diagnosis can be made early enough in a pregnancy to consider termination if that is felt to be the most desirable alternative. No testing or counseling service can guarantee that a child will be normal, and none should pressure potential parents to make any particular decision.

The usual procedure for prenatal diagnosis currently involves three stages. First, the people who are concerned about the potential risk of genetic disease should schedule counseling. This counseling will always include interviews about the history of medical conditions and premature mortality in the families involved. When the disorder in question is very rare or complicated, such as some of the disorders involving biochemcial deficiencies, consultations with a specialist in medical genetics may be advisable. Some disorders can be diagnosed through family history information or tests for the "carrier" condition in relatives. Others cannot be diagnosed with certainty through any currently known procedures, although progress is being reported for more and more of these conditions. Many conditions can best be diagnosed through amniocentesis—a minor surgical procedure conducted during mid-pregnancy, in which a small amount of amniotic fluid is withdrawn from the uterus, and fetal cells in that fluid are cultured in special diagnostic laboratories. After several weeks, enough genetic material has grown to permit a search for defects.

Amniocentesis is recommended whenever there is concern about increased risk of genetic or developmental defects in a pregnancy. Most physicians include all women over 35 in the "risk" group, which also includes parents who have borne previous children with defects, and potential parents with a family history of concern.

The risks of amniocentesis are few if the procedure is done by experienced, specialized professionals. Ideally, it is performed between the fourteenth and sixteenth weeks of pregnancy, when the enlarging uterus can be properly felt through the abdominal wall. Sound wave visualization of the fetus (usually called ultrasound or sonography) is used to make sure of the position of the fetus in the amniotic fluid, so that the device used for withdrawal of some fluid does not inadvertently contact the fetus or the placenta. Although most patients experience some slight discomfort during the procedure, it is usually no more than that connected with other injections; afterward, they may have some contractions similar to menstrual discomfort. The risk of miscarriage is very small when the procedure is performed in centers that specialize in it. Some few pregnancies will miscarry at this stage of pregnancy regardless of whether amniocentesis is done. An extremely large collaborative amniocentesis registry project analyzed more than 1,000 women who had the test and compared them to 992 pregnant women who had not.[32] The study found no increased risk of miscarriage or complications in the tested women.

Assuming that the procedure is done, as it should be, in the center where the diagnostic laboratory is located, there is only a 5 to 10 percent risk that the removed cells may not grow successfully in the laboratory and that the test may have to be repeated. (If the fluid must be transported some distance, this risk increases, although successful cultures have been grown on samples flown more than 6,000 miles for diagnosis.)

The vast majority of amniocentesis results indicate no abnormalities in the structural or genetic conditions that can be diagnosed from this procedure, even though the potential parents who undergo the procedure represent a high-risk group. Although not all defects or abnormalities can be diagnosed from these procedures, many of the most common ones—such as Down syndrome—can, and the positive news from such testing can mean considerable relief for many potential parents.

The news is not always positive, of course, which makes the third stage of prenatal tesing especially valuable. In this stage, parents have the opportunity to discuss the test findings with a counselor who is knowledgeable about the details of the risk involved, including the likelihood of severe defects (and what kinds) and the probable future for the child and the family if the child is born. Many genetically caused biochemical defects, for example, can be treated, sometimes even during the pregnancy, and although the defect cannot be cured, a relatively normal development can be achieved with proper diet or medication.

Most parents who receive bad news, however, choose to terminate that pregnancy through abortion; most of these then achieve a subsequent normal, successful pregnancy and delivery. Even in families with dominant hereditary abnormalities, the odds for any one child are only 50 percent, so some positive, normal results are possible. As one researcher related:

Joanne was eighteen and unmarried. When she found herself pregnant by her fiance she came for genetic counseling. Her pregnancy had already advanced to 16 weeks. The reason for seeking counseling was that her sister had Down's syndrome. She was therefore worried that her child might inherit it. It was not known at that time which kind of Down's syndrome her sister had; the very uncommon hereditary form or the common nonhereditary type.

Because there is a very significant risk of carrying a fetus with Down's syndrome for those individuals who carry the hereditary form of mongolism, amniocentesis and prenatal genetic studies were provided immediately.

Some two weeks later, when the results came in, it turned out that her fetus had the hereditary type. This eighteen-year-old prospective mother and her fiance then elected to have an abortion, which was done forthwith and the affected fetus found as predicted. Blood studies for chromosomal analysis on her, performed prior to abortion, had shown also that Joanne was a translocation carrier of the disease, and later we confirmed that her sister and mother were carriers of hereditary Down's syndrome too.

Less than one year later, now married, Joanne again presented herself for prenatal studies—this time three months pregnant. At the recommended time (14 to 16 weeks of pregnancy) an amniocentesis was performed. We were able to show on this occasion that the second fetus had normal chromosomes and was a male.

On the very day that this normal result was provided, she indicated that she had been exposed to what sounded like classic German measles when she was three months pregnant. Immediate blood studies disclosed that she had indeed contracted the infection. Therefore, another amniocentesis was performed between 21 and 22 weeks of pregnancy and the German measles virus was found in the amniotic fluid cells. The parents elected—for the second time—to abort this pregnancy as well. Studies on the aborted fetus showed severe fetal infection by German measles virus, confirming the prenatal diagnosis. As we have said, children born after rubella infection in the womb may have major birth defects including mental retardation, cataracts, heart defects, stunted growth, and deafness. (Amniocentesis is not usually recommended for mothers who are not immune to rubella and have been exposed to it while pregnant.)

Some months later she arrived with a third pregnancy. Amniocentesis this time revealed one amniotic fluid cell with a ring-shaped chromosome (which is decidedly abnormal) in about 60 cells analyzed. We indicated that we (and others) did not know the meaning of this observation and did not believe it likely that the fetus was affected, but could not be sure. The young couple, having already been through so much, decided to keep the pregnancy. They had their daughter as predicted, and she looked like a sound baby. Chromosome studies on both blood and skin revealed a normal pattern![33]

If the nature of the genetic problem is such that it can continue with subsequent pregnancies, most counselors also discuss future considerations and alternatives, including additional detection studies, adoption, or artificial insemination by a donor if the hereditary trait is in the father's family. More recently, there is also the option of a donor arrangement for the maternal side of the couple; this may be for genetic reasons or, more often, because of some medical problem of the mother that makes her unable to carry a pregnancy successfully. It should be emphasized again, however, that the role of prenatal diagnosis and counseling is to provide potential parents with as much information as possible, so that they can decide what to do with a future that is theirs alone. It is not the role of the professional counselor to insinuate his or her own eugenic, religious, or racial views into the decision process.

Many parents complain that the timing of amniocentesis in a pregnancy limits its maximum potential benefit. When a major problem is not discovered until twenty weeks into a pregnancy, the developing child is already a presence whose existence and movement cannot be taken lightly. Efforts are under way to develop safe but accurate tests that can be performed much earlier in a pregnancy, so that decisions can be made at a stage when their long-range effects can be anticipated more realistically and when the risks of termination, if that is chosen, are less traumatic.

In June 1983, researchers reported successful early test results on a procedure called chorion biopsy.[34] This test, which can be done as early as the eighth week of pregnancy, involves taking a small snip of tissue from the chorion, an early precursor of the placenta. Tests for genetic abnormalities can be done immediately, and the results can be available in days instead of weeks.

Two other kinds of tests that can be part of prenatal diagnostic procedures are increasingly becoming routine in most testing centers. The first kind involves biochemical studies of the amniotic fluid itself. Some developmental defects can be detected by very abnormal levels of some components of the amniotic fluid. The most common test of this kind is for alpha-fetoprotein (AFP), a relatively rare protein manufactured by the fetal liver. Ordinarily, levels of this protein in the amniotic fluid are low, but when there are so-called "open defects" of the brain or the spinal cord, AFP leaks directly into the fluid and is therefore found at much higher levels. Other conditions of grave risk to the fetus, even fetal death, also raise levels of this protein; thus, although a diagnostic finding of high AFP levels may not indicate which specific problem exists, it is probable that the problem is a major one.

The use of ultrasound (sonography) is most useful when gross physical birth defects are the concern. In such cases, there may not be a genetic cause, so amniocentesis will yield normal results. Missing or deformed limbs, gross malformation of the head or internal organs, and developmental problems can be diagnosed with ultrasound. The procedure is not invasive; it works by the passage of sound waves through the uterus, which are then transformed into a screen image that looks somewhat like an X ray but does not subject the mother or fetus to radiation. Sonography may be used several times during a pregnancy, especially when multiple births are suspected or when there are questions about the normal rate of development of the fetus. For many older mothers, sonography can provide the reassuring news that a uterus that appears to be "too large" for an early stage of pregnancy, thus perhaps indicating twins, is in fact a normal-sized single fetus plus some fibroid development.

Risk to the Child

The potential effects of later childbearing in terms of risk to the child, in order of increasing concern, are as follows:

Low birth weight or prematurity

Birth defects, congenital or chromosomal (hereditary)

Failure to survive the prenatal period (death after twenty-eight weeks of gestation through four weeks after delivery).

These unfortunate occurrences can afflict parents of any age, but they tend to be rare. Figure 3–1 shows recent findings on these risks for children born to mothers in various age groups. The information provided in the figure is reassuring in several ways. First, even for the most frequent problem, low birth weight, older mothers are only slightly more likely than younger ones to deliver premature infants. Approximately 6 percent of all births fall into this category; the percentage for mothers from 35 to 39, is 9 percent, and it is only slightly higher for mothers 40 and older. As noted earlier, many premature births among older mothers are due to the increased proportion of multiple births.

Many birth defects are very rare regardless of maternal age. Fewer than 1 percent of all births are children with major defects. This proportion is higher for older mothers, but it does not exceed 2 percent of all births, even those to mothers 40 and older. This means that even allowing for the increased risk of some chromosomal abnormalities, such as Down syndrome in children born to older parents, the total risk of any serious birth defect is still less than 2 of every 100 births.

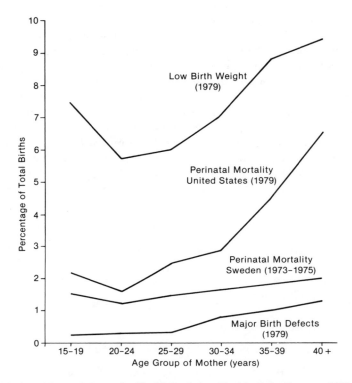

Source: U.S. data: National Center for Health Statistics, *Vital Statistics Reports,* 1979. Swedish data: O. Meirik, B. Smedby, A. Ericson. "Impact of Changing Age and Parity Distribution of Mothers on Perinatal Mortality in Sweden, 1953–1975." *International Journal of Epidemiology,* 1979.

Note: Perinatal mortality includes death after the twenty-eighth week of pregnancy through four weeks after delivery. Major birth defects include both congenital and chromosomal anomalies.

Figure 3–1. Risk to the Child, by Age Group of Mother

Finally, figure 3–1 also shows that perinatal mortality in the United States averages less than 3 percent of all births; the risk increases to over 4 percent for women aged 35 to 39 and 6 percent for women 40 and older. It is very important to note, however, that this increased perinatal mortality for older parents is not necessary or inevitable, illustrated by the data presented for Sweden. The Swedish data are for the years 1973 through 1975; this means that, even ten years ago, some countries with more thorough prenatal care and monitoring and better personal health habits were achieving survival rates for infants born to older mothers that were as good as those for younger mothers. We can do as well in this country.

Summary: Assessing Your Medical and Genetic Risk

This chapter has discussed the medical and genetic risks currently known to be associated with pregnancy, both those that are higher for people over 35 and those that are not. Much of the previously published information about increased risk with age might have been true at some time in the past, but it is unlikely to be true any longer. With increased knowledge, improved medical care, and a new generation of parents who are healthier at 30, 35, 40, and even older, than their counterparts in previous generations, our current estimation of risk for this age group has decreased dramatically.

For births at any age, the chances for complications or genetic predisposition to serious birth defects are less than 5 in 100; with the few exceptions noted in this chapter, the risk is no different for parents over 35 who are in good health. Even for people with conditions that can cause problems, such as heart disease, diabetes, or hypertension, current high-risk obstetric care can reduce the chances of complications much more than was possible even five years ago—and more progress is being reported all the time.

Furthermore, advanced diagnostic and counseling techniques can provide information on genetically caused disorders and major birth defects during a pregnancy, thereby allowing prospective parents to choose whether or not to continue a pregnancy.

People of any age who are considering parenthood have an obligation to themselves and to their possible children to examine the medical aspects of this decision with some care and planning. The serious potential parent should consider all of the following factors before making a decision about parenthood, or at least before beginning a pregnancy:

1. Assess your own health and that of your partner. The current state of the parents' health is the most important predictor of the success or complications of pregnancy. This assessment should include measurement of your physical health by a professional, with particular attention to those diseases that are more frequent with increased age, such as hypertension and diabetes. In addition, consider your own role in establishing and maintaining health through your own behavior, including diet, exercise, use of alcohol and other drugs, and smoking.

2. Assess your environment and that of your partner. Most occupational exposures are avoidable, but avoidance may require advance planning and

even occupational change. Other potentially harmful exposures, such as X rays, can be deferred or avoided.

3. If you are over 35 or have a family history of concern, consider the possibility and availability of genetic counseling. An examination of family history (and testing, if advisable) can be done before a pregnancy. The resources to provide this information are becoming more widely available all the time.

4. Arrange a thorough diagnostic workup, and develop a trusting but communicative relationship with a professional who can advise you regarding contraception and conception. Be sure that this professional has the time to discuss all your concerns and the resources available to you. A great deal of unnecessary concern on the part of potential older parents is based on lack of knowledge.

Notes

1. M. Fabe and N. Wikler, *Up Against the Clock: Career Women Speak on the Choice to Have Children* (New York: Random House, 1979).

2. S.P. Rubin, *It's Not Too Late For a Baby: For Men and Women Over 35* (Englewood Cliffs, N.J.: Prentice-Hall, 1980).

3. A.H. deCherney and G.S. Berkowitz, "Female Fecundity and Age," *New England Journal of Medicine* 306(1982):424–426.

4. N.B. Ryder, "Letter to the Editor," *New England Journal of Medicine* 307(1982):273.

5. Federation CECOS, D. Schwartz, and M.J. Mayaux, "Female Fecundity as a Function of Age," *New England Journal of Medicine* 306(1982):404–407.

6. G.E. Hendershot, "Maternal Age and Overdue Conceptions," *American Journal of Public Health* 74(1984):35–38.

7. Z. Stein and J. Kline, Smoking, Alcohol, and Reproduction," *American Journal of Public Health* 73(1983):1154–1156.

8. U.S. Department of Health, Education and Welfare, Office of the Assistant Secretary of Health and Surgeon General, *Healthy People: The Surgeon General's Report on Health Promotion and Disease Prevention,* DHEW Publication No. (PHS)79–55071 (Washington, D.C.: U.S. Government Printing Office, 1979).

9. R. Brent and M. Harris (eds.), *Prevention of Embryonic, Fetal, and Perinatal Disease,* DHEW Pub. No. (NIH)76–853 (Bethesda, Md.: National Institutes of Health, 1976).

10. H. Kalter and J. Warkany, "Congenital Malformations: Etiologic Factors and Their Role in Prevention," *New England Journal of Medicine* 308(1983): 424–431, 491–497.

11. H. Tuchmann-Duplessis, "Teratogenic Risk," in D. Mattison (ed.), *Reproductive Toxicology: Progress in Clinical and Biological Research* (New York: Liss, 1983), pp. 242–260.

12. P.J. Aselton and S. Stergachis, "Increasing Incidence of Ectopic Pregnancy,"

Journal of the American Medical Association 251(1984):469; D.M. Glebatis and D.T. Janerich, "Ectopic Pregnancies in Upstate New York," *Journal of the American Medical Association* 248(1983):1730–1735.

13. G.L. Rubin, H.B. Peterson, S.F. Dorfman, et al., "Ectopic Pregnancy in the United States: 1970 through 1978," *Journal of the American Medical Association* 249(1983):1725–1729.

14. J.A. Merrill, "Endometriosis," in D. Danforth (ed.), *Obstetrics and Gynecology*, 4th ed. (Philadelphia, Harper & Row, 1982), pp. 1004–1014.

15. Stein and Kline, "Smoking, Alcohol, and Reproduction." See also "Editorial: Alcohol and Spontaneous Abortion," *Lancet* 2(1980):188.

16. D.U. Himmelberger, B.W. Brown, Jr., and E.N. Cohen, "Cigarette Smoking during Pregnancy and the Occurrence of Spontaneous Abortion and Congenital Abnormality," *American Journal of Epidemiology* 108(1978):470–479; J. Kline, Z. Stein, M. Susser, et al., "Smoking: A Risk Factor for Spontaneous Abortion," *New England Journal of Medicine* 297(1977):793–796.

17. J.L. Kitzmiller, "Diabetic Pregnancy and Perinatal Morbidity," *American Journal of Obstetrics and Gynecology* 131(1978):560–566.

18. J. Pederson and L. Molsted-Pedersen, "Congenital Malformations: The Possible Role of Diabetes Care Outside Pregnancy," in R.S. Beard and J.J. Hoed (eds.), *Pregnancy Metabolism, Diabetes, and the Fetus,* CIBA Foundation Symposium No. 63 (Amsterdam: Exerpta Medica, 1979).

19. J.A. Pritchard and P.C. Macdonald, *Williams Obstetrics,* 16th ed. (New York: Appleton-Century-Crofts, 1976), p. 531.

20. D.M. Reed and F.J. Stanley (eds.), *The Epidemiology of Prematurity,* Proceedings of a working conference held at NICHD-NIH, Bethesda, Md., November 1976 (Baltimore and Munich: Urban & Schwarzenburg, 1977), pp. 25–26.

21. Pritchard and Macdonald, *Williams Obstetrics,* pp. 415–421.

22. J.B. Hardy and E.D. Mellits, "Relationship of Low Birth Weight to Maternal Characteristics of Age, Parity, Education and Body Size," in Reed and Stanley, *The Epidemiology of Prematurity,* pp. 105–117.

23. Rubin, *It's Not Too Late,* pp. 212–225.

24. D. Mattison (ed.), *Reproductive Toxicology: Progress in Clinical and Biological Research* (New York: Liss, 1983).

25. Centers for Disease Control, "Current Trends: Rubella and Congenital Rubella, United States, 1980–1983," *Morbidity and Mortality Weekly Report* 32 (October 7, 1983):505–509.

26. P. Placek, S. Taffel, and M. Moien, "Caesarian Section Delivery Rates: United States, 1981," *American Journal of Public Health* 73(1983):861–862.

27. Rubin, *It's Not Too Late,* p. 224.

28. I. Kern, "No Better Time: The Choice of Parenting over 35," Paper presented at the National Association of Social Workers Professional Symposium, Washington, D.C., November 22, 1983.

29. E.B. Hook and E.M. Chambers, "Estimated Rates of Down Syndrome in Live Births by One Year Maternal Age Intervals for Mothers Aged 20–49 in a New York State Study," in D. Bergsma and B.R. Lowry (eds.), *Numerical Taxonomy of Birth Defects and Polygenic Disorders* (New York: National Foundation—March of Dimes, 1977), pp. 123–141.

30. National Institute of Child Health and Human Development, National Institutes of Health, *Antenatal Diagnosis: Report of a Consensus Development Conference* (Washington, D.C.: U.S. Department of Health, Education and Welfare, 1979).

31. Based on the experience of the University of California San Francisco Medical Center, and consistent with other major American and Canadian studies. See National Institute of Child Health and Human Development, *Antenatal Diagnosis: Report of a Consensus Development Conference,* p. 1–66.

32. K.J. Roghmann and R.A. Doherty, "Reassurance through Prenatal Diagnosis and Willingness to Bear Children after Age 35," *American Journal of Public Health* 73(1983):760–762.

33. A. Milunsky, *Know Your Genes* (Boston: Houghton Mifflin, 1977), pp. 166–167.

34. G. Kolata, "First Trimester Prenatal Diagnosis," *Science* 221 (September 9, 1983):1031–1032.

4
Making a Choice in a Specific Social Context

This is the first of two chapters intended to encourage a personal, detailed assessment of the components of your current situation and your readiness to consider the changes in that situation that could follow your decision to be or not to be a parent. For most of us, it is easier to assess our current social circumstances than it is to look inward and understand our personal hopes and concerns, so this chapter will begin by considering the daily social context in which you live.

One way to begin is by considering the social roles you already perform regularly. Attached to each role are some expectations for its performance and for the costs and rewards associated with that activity. We will assess these roles in three ways. The first assessment will be in terms of each role's necessity to you. Some roles may be essential; others may only be necessary to meet more general needs, and they may have alternatives that could be considered in planning life changes. Second, we will consider how these roles might compete or conflict with the demands of the added role of either parent or permanently childless person. Such potential areas of incompatibility are often the reason people feel unable to make a final choice about parenthood. Finally, it will be useful to try to predict possible changes that might be necessary in your current social situation if a choice is made either for parenthood or for a permanently childfree future. The roles to be discussed here may be performed by men or by women. They may also be held by people in conventional or nonconventional relationships or those in potential single-parent situations. Since single parenthood is a venture with greater potential risk, however, we will discuss the single-parent perspective further later in the chapter.

The Role of Worker

The role of worker includes all the activities people describe when they are asked what they "do." It includes typical employee/employer situations in which you are paid for doing specific tasks for a fixed time period per day in a limited location, but it also includes independent or self-employment, in the sense of working in areas that are less specified in tasks, hours, location, or certainty of financial compensation for effort expended. Regardless of your job title or whether you think others would call what you do a "job," consider the following aspects of the work you do:

1. What do you produce from your work? (This may be some kind of service rather than a specific product.)
2. Must your work be done in a specific setting? Can any of it be done at home?
3. Does your work have specific time requirements—not just regular working hours, but evenings, or overtime during crises or in certain seasons?
4. Do you consider your work a career? Are you on a progressive path of increasing responsibility and prestige, which may require that you spend extra time in preparation or that you relocate to progress up that ladder?
5. How important are you to others in the performance of their work? Are you essential or depended upon?
6. How much does your work role overlap with other roles in your life? Do you work pretty much alone, keeping your work separate from the rest of your life, or are your co-workers also your friends or family members?
7. What kinds of rewards does your worker role provide to you? Are they only financial, or do they also include less tangible rewards, such as self-esteem because of the type of work you do or because you are a reliable, superior worker who is depended upon?

Each of these dimensions of your work role has implications for your decision about parenthood. Since work time accounts for the majority of most people's hours, except for sleeping time (and you can be sure your sleeping time will change drastically for some period if you choose parenthood!), it is the area in which the greatest impact of change may be felt. Although you may assume that important changes will occur only for those who choose to become parents, it has been found that work role changes may occur whichever way the decision goes. Women who decide in their thirties to remain permanently childless and seek permanent contraception through sterilization often report the same experience as women who finally accept, after years of trying, that they cannot conceive a child. Women in both groups report a release of tension and anxiety because this aspect of their lives is no longer uncertain; this feeling of release often is channeled into personal or career development gains that had been deferred.

The more usual situation, however, is a concern about potential conflicts between the expectations of the work role and those of parenthood. The extent and type of potential conflict can take as many forms as the nature of the fit between this pair of roles for each person. At the most traditional level, some people foresee very little conflict between the two roles. It is possible to expect that there will be separate work time (weekdays) and parenting time (some evenings and some part of weekends) if you assume that all of the following conditions will be true when you become a parent: you will never have to take work home; someone else will have the primary responsibility for the bulk of "family work," such as cooking, bathing, day care, sick care, and the like; and someone else will handle all middle-of-the-night demands. If a person who sees the parenthood role in these terms chooses to become a parent, someone else had better be prepared to handle most of the changes that occur when a child is added to people's daily life. Arthur and Libby Coleman note that this traditional "sky father" perspective—of one parent going off to conquer the world and "bring home the bacon"—only works if there is a complementary "earth mother" caretaker, whose role is to manage the myriad home front details.[1]

This traditional separation of roles works best when the partner who relinquishes the work role with the advent of parenthood does so willingly. The majority of people who negotiate work and parenthood by giving up the former for the latter, at least temporarily, are still women. Recently, however, increasing numbers of men who have tired of the excessive demands and limited rewards of their work roles choose to stay home and be the primary parent, at least for a while. Regardless of gender, such people are among those who believe that during the early years of parenthood, the roles of worker and parent cannot mesh in the same daily existence.

Even some people who apparently have been successful at combining both roles would not necessarily do so again if given the choice. Actress Meryl Streep announced at the release of her critically acclaimed film, *Silkwood,* that she was taking a year off from her career to coincide with the arrival of her second child. When asked if she worried about what would happen to her career in the interim, she replied: "No, not at all; successful women are people whose lives have more of an ebb and flow."[2] She reported that her own work pattern alternated between periods of intense activity and times when she needed to pull away. It was not that she lost interest in either career or parenthood; rather, it was impossible for her to have two very young children and also be away on location. For her, the essential nature of early parenthood took precedence over other choices, or over trying to divide herself between them and still do justice to both.

It is an oversimplification to state that work roles, especially those of the career type, cannot mesh with the role of parent. Each person must realistically assess how demanding, how rewarding, and how inflexible the work role is in his or her life. In part, this assessment can be done in terms of the factual information derived from the seven questions you were asked to help you consider your work role. If your work is inflexible in hours, location, and the like, there may be little that can be changed to accommodate to the added demands of parenthood. This is the current situation of millions of working parents, and their continuing major problem is finding child care that is of sufficient quality to earn their trust yet is available for the hours they need at a price they can afford. It is also true, however, that those jobs in which unpredictability is built in, requiring odd working hours and extra time, may be even more difficult to accommodate to the demands of the parent role. The great majority of child care arrangements have relatively inflexible schedules, not including evenings and weekends.

In the developing years of a career, the extra demands of a job may be the most extreme, often serving the added function of identifying those aspirants who demonstrate the extra level of dedication that can earn more rapid advancement. Many careers, for women as well as for men, also require a willingness to travel or relocate if necessary. Sometimes the added expectations of a career are less visible, but they may be just as costly in terms of time available for other activities. Many professional occupations, and those in rapidly developing fields such as high technology, fashion, and various kinds of research, require extra, unpaid hours of reading and preparation just to keep up with new developments. Many people thrive in such exciting and fast-moving environments, but some have found it very difficult to mesh them with the demands of parenthood.

In *The Two Paycheck Marriage,* Caroline Bird warns that such fast-moving careers make parenthood particularly risky for women whose husbands are also on career paths.[3] Her warning is directed primarily at women who take time off to have a child. If they do not work at all for a time, they not only can expect to lose their place on the ladder to the top, but they may never be able to get back on the ladder again. The experience of Supreme Court Justice Sandra Day O'Connor, however, did not follow this pattern, perhaps because the law is not a fast-moving career path compared to some others. After graduating third in her law school class at Stanford, O'Connor was unable to obtain a job as a lawyer; her only job offer was as a legal secretary. After working as a lawyer for a number of years, she did not practice law for six years while her children were young. During that time, however, she helped start the state bar's legal referral service, sat on the local zoning commission, and wrote questions for the state bar exam. She returned to full-time practice in 1965, and the rest is history. In a recent interview in the *American Bar Association Journal,* she said:

> For women lawyers who want to have families, the ideal thing is to be able to work part time and perhaps to leave practice altogether and then later go back. . . . That's very hard to do because you are not advancing at the same pace as your colleagues. But I think by and large most women discover they actually can re-enter the profession and they can make up for lost ground.[4]

From the available evidence, there does seem to be some difference in the experience of those who choose parenthood within a career at younger ages and those who do so further along the career path, when they are older. In general, the younger the age at parenthood, the more terms such as *guilt, anxiety,* and *conflict* are used to describe the early years of parenthood. Younger working parents report that neither role's demands and expectations could be met adequately and that the balance between career and parenthood was both tense and fragile, especially in the face of demands for additional work time or the need for alternative child care arrangements due to illness.

People who delayed parenthood until they were older however, more often report that although there are still complications and competition for scarce time resources between career and parenthood, there is often less conflict involved. There is less ego involvement and more challenge to arrangements and scheduling, which often turn out to be easier because of greater financial resources. Those who take some work time off to begin parenthood after delaying for some time still say that parenthood can interfere with a career, but they are also more likely to add that it *should* do so. For example, in a study of twenty women who became first-time parents after having been profitably and enjoyably employed as professionals for some time, all of the women finally chose to stay out of the work force, at least for the first year, for various reasons: readiness to take some time off, the importance of being continuously available during their children's early development, or just the pleasure and satisfactions of early parenthood.[5] Although not all of the women had anticipated a total change, the importance of their new role had come to take precedence over the old one, at least temporarily.

Taking time off, and thereby avoiding potential conflict between occupational and parental roles, is the most satisfactory solution for people who feel strongly positive about both roles but also have decided that they are unwilling or unable to perform in both simultaneously, especially early in their parenthood. As one set of parents told me, they had done the same in the early years of their career development; that is, they had focused solely on getting their professional lives off to the best possible start. To them, parenthood was equally important and deserving of an equally strong and focused level of attention. They had included in their planning a period prior to and during pregnancy when they could accumulate some financial reserves against the anticipated unemployment. They also noted that the reduction in expenses for things curtailed due to parenthood, such as travel and entertainment, helped offset the increased parenthood expenses.

Although this couple's carefully planned arrangements were working out "pretty well" midway in the first year, they expressed dissatisfaction with two aspects of their work situations. First, both would have preferred to have the father take some time off from work just after the birth. His employment situation did not recognize "paternity leave" as legitimate, however, and the only way he had been able to take time off was by using vacation time. Furthermore, he resented the continuing necessity of working extra hours during sporadic rush periods at work. He avoided such extra work as often as he felt he could, but he was aware that his disappearances were noticed by those who had a voice in his promotion chances.

His partner had avoided these dilemmas by taking the first year off; in doing so, however, she had become vulnerable to the complementary side of the problem. Her maximum allowable maternity leave, three months, was on the generous side; to take a year off, however, she had to resign her position, and her employer was not required to rehire her when she was ready to return. She knew that her professional skills were not going to deteriorate in a year, and she had an excellent performance record, but both partners were concerned about how difficult it would be for her to find an equivalent position when she wanted to return to work.

The experience of this couple is not unusual, except that both of them were involved in planning and implementing their decisions and they both would have preferred to share more equally the changes associated with early parenthood. Unfortunately, the combination of circumstances that permits more equal sharing of the added demands and rewards of early parenthood is still quite rare; as more and more potential parents demand them, however, changes are beginning to occur.

Although taking a prolonged or indefinite leave from work is the best solution for potential role conflict for some people, most potential parents say that they would need to continue to work. Financial considerations rank high in the reasons given, but a much more important dimension in terms of parenthood decisions is the importance of work itself. Any job is more than just completion of tasks; it may also include responsibility, recognition, accomplishment, prestige, and social support. Before you can decide how much you feel you can afford to change or give up a job, you must consider how much such rewards mean to you.

At one extreme, your assessment may indicate that your work brings monetary rewards but few others. If that is the case, the likelihood of conflict with the added demands of parenthood could be low, especially if your work situation does not conflict logistically, in terms of hours and the like. People who assess their work situations this way often find alternative part-time work situations, so that there is still some income available.

At the other extreme is the person whose work is engrossing and rewarding, regardless of income. More than a few parents report that they would not have chosen parenthood if they had known of the insoluble conflicts between the demands of career and those of parenthood. One such woman, quoted in Fabe and Wikler, said:

> Women who are truly ambitious and absorbed in their work should not ruin
> their chances for a satisfying career just because they feel they should have

children, or that they would miss something if they didn't . . . nothing I read discussed that one simply ought not to have children if one is really caught up in a career and feels strongly about the way one wants to live one's life. . . . There is a strong taboo in our culture where we do not admit publicly that having children is ever a mistake, or that they are not beneficial.[6]

Assessment in hindsight is of limited help, of course, to people who are facing a decision now. Although there is no direct experience that is identical to parenthood, try to imagine a situation that is unpredictably demanding and exhausting (as well as rewarding) and that would overlap the time and energy you now devote to work. If you find that your work is truly absorbing, to the point that you are angered or irritated by interruptions, then the multitudinous, unpredictable demands of parenthood will not be easy for you. If you and your partner are both willing workaholics, choosing parenthood as well may bring serious conflict to your relationship as each of you struggles to maintain some level of preparenthood productivity.

Most of us fall somewhere between these extremes. Our work provides some rewards and recognition, but we also enjoy other things in life. We take our responsibilities seriously and are good at what we do, but we also daydream occasionally of time that is more free. From the majority of women and men in this middle range, a self-description like this is nearly always accompanied by the expression of the other major concern that lurks along the boundary between the worlds of work and parenthood: Does a child need a full-time parent at home for at least the early period of childhood? What is the effect of a parent's continuing to work on the healthy growth and development of the child? Do children of working mothers develop more social and emotional problems or later problems in school?

These questions have been around for a long time, but information is now available from a great deal of carefully designed research that provides sufficient evidence to lay certain myths to rest.[7] Some children do have problems, of course, but these problems are associated with the psychological status of the parents, not their employment status. Parents who are unhappy and anxious about working communicate this anxiety and distress to their children. Conversely, parents who are bored and depressed staying at home full-time also communicate this to their children. Studies in many countries have demonstrated that even young children thrive in day care situations and can bond successfully to more than one caregiver, if the care is relatively continuous over time. So long as the family and the day care situations are stable and supportive, there are few differences in emotional or social development or problems between infants and toddlers in day care and those who stay at home.

If anything, recent evidence has accumulated in favor of the positive aspects of families with nontraditional parenting arrangements. Families with working mothers and those with fathers who are also nurturing have been observed to encourage development in their children that is relatively more rapid, more socially outgoing, and more adaptable. Children who grow in families where there is sharing of both working and nurturing roles tend to relate more positively to others and to hold fewer rigid stereotypes about male and female roles. Researchers in child development suggest that the current generation of children, having grown up in families where both parents work, may well have different attitudes about both work and their own roles in life.[8] The next generation of women may be less troubled about pursuing both masculine and feminine endeavors, because they will have had role models to observe and emulate who have integrated both. For boys, having mothers (and, increasingly, fathers) who are both achieving and nurturing can lead to recognition and acceptance of both capacities in themselves and in women in their adult life.

Even more extensive research on children of school age has been reviewed and summarized by Hoffman and Nye,[9] who conclude that there are no differences between children of working versus nonworking mothers in emotional problems, school achievement, or social adjustment. They report, further, that some studies indicate that children whose mothers work have higher motivation toward achievement and higher educational and occupational goals. Daughters, especially, of working mothers demonstrate these characteristics and are more likely than their peers to cite their mothers as the persons they most admire.

Clearly, from the examples presented here, there are many possibilities for choice in assessing the potential for parenthood within the context of a personal assessment of one's work role. Some people prefer to have their work change as little as possible; in that case, the choice can still range from permanent nonparenthood to parenthood with extensive and reliable child care as an absolute necessity. Others may decide to wait longer to make a choice about parenthood, until there can be more flexibility in their work roles or until some mutually agreeable and feasible sharing arrangement can be worked out to meet the anticipated added demands if parenthood is chosen. Finally, some people, after completing both a social and a personal assessment, may decide that although their work situation is far from optimal, parenthood would not be an escape from facing necessary work-related changes.

Family Roles

During the process of evaluating your work role, you have come to realize that some issues in the work versus parenthood analysis were strongly affected by your expectations about other roles in your life, especially the role of family member. Of all the roles to be assessed, your family role will be most definitely affected by your parenthood choice. More than one role is involved here; your role as son or daughter as well as your role as mate are influenced by and, in turn, will influence your decisions about parenthood. What you need to assess are two separate but very much intertwined family roles—the one in which you grew up and the one in which you are presently a member of a pair (or larger group) of your own choosing. Even people who no longer have living parents will find this assessment valuable, because so much of what we are and what we have chosen to do with our lives is in response to parental influences, even if only in reaction against those influences. From the earliest and most continuous of roles, we all begin to form our own convictions of what family life should be like and what roles family members should fill to make that kind of family life possible.

In the most basic terms, a family provides the necessities of existence, such as nourishment and rest, and it also provides a base for intimacy and love. Family adult roles include provision of those basics, although there are differences in definitions of who among a family's adults provides each of them. Most of us grew up in relatively traditional families, in which the father role included primary responsibility for going out into the world and providing for the family financially and the mother role, whether or not it included outside employment, was primarily to provide nurturance and daily guidance in the myriad small details of the household and personal tasks of family life. Even within this traditional division of family labor, there was a great deal of room for variation in other aspects of family roles. The relative balance of power, for example, could vary from the patriarchal type, in which the father made all the rules and was the final enforcement authority and everyone else was to be obedient and/or supportive, to the almost purely matriarchal type, in which the mother controlled all the real family power. (This type was made infamous by the stereotype of the Jewish mother.)

Similarly, the extent of participation expected in family life could range from the most limited, providing basic essentials only, to one in which generations shared most activities, both necessary and recreational ones. The pattern of participation is also associated with another key aspect of family life—the type and extent of nurturance provided. One of the more unfortunate stereotypes in this culture is that the capacity to nurture is inherently female. Evidence from other cultures and from observation of animal behavior suggests, instead, that nurturing can be performed by members of either sex and, conversely, that not all females are inherently nurturing. You may know, as I do, some couples in which the man is more nurturing than his mate, as well as some in which both members seem to be high or low in this characteristic. People differ in their capacities both to need and to provide nurturance, yet too many of us are quite unaware of our own level of need for and ability to provide this essentially intimate activity; we rely, instead, on sex-role stereotypes of what is expected. Traditionally, these stereotypes claim that men neither need nor provide much nurturance, that women need some and can provide a great deal of it, and that children need a great deal until they grow into boys who need less and girls who need more. In your own family, you may recall that boys were cuddled less than girls were and that cuddling of boys stopped earlier.

Now consider the division of labor in family tasks, family power, and nurturance in the family setting where you grew up and in your current family situation. As you review the following questions, assess, in addition, the relative satisfaction of each family member with his or her expected role. Consider, also the extent to which you are replicating or reacting against what you remember from your own family pattern in childhood.

1. Who went out into the world to work and earn the money to pay the bills?
2. Who was the final judge on family rules and infractions of them?
3. Who helped with the family work—cleaning, shopping, minor repairs, meal preparation, and the like?
4. Who attended family occasions—birthdays, graduations, recitals?
5. Who participated in family recreation time—picnics, camping, and the like?
6. Who provided nurturance, comforting, and cuddling, and who was entitled to receive it?

Most of us find ourselves with present family roles that differ from those we observed while we were growing up, at least in part because our social environment has changed. A social system in which the majority of adult women work and in which a significant proportion of adults are still trying to come to a decision about parenthood after age 30 is very different from the social environment of even a generation ago. Contemporary intimate relationships are more likely to have moved toward a mixing of traditionally defined male and female role tasks; both partners may go out and work, and both (or neither) may perform the family work of housecleaning, cooking, and the like. Interdependence, or relative independence, is more typical than the separate and unequal male and female roles of the past. This does not mean, however, that most relationships have moved entirely away from the traditional model or that they should do so if the partners are more comfortable otherwise. National opinion polls still indicate that most people feel that the male partner should have a higher-status job and should make more money if both partners work.[10] Furthermore, household tasks are still taking far more of women's nonworking hours than of men's, even when both partners work full-time.

However your family role tasks are currently divided, try to predict what might happen to the present balance if a totally dependent family member were to be added. First, you may be sure that the readjustment strains would be very high initially, as the demands for care and nurturance explode in even the best-prepared intimate relationships. In the extensive and often contradictory literature on parenthood, this is one theme that appears to be unanimous. Family structural arrangements—all of those longstanding ways of meeting everyday needs—will be severely disrupted. Studies of initial parenthood indicate that virtually all first-time parents report some level of crisis in adjusting to a first child, and the majority report that the crisis is extensive or severe.[11] Furthermore, this assessment of crisis is not affected by the quality of the relationship before parenthood or by the extent of wanting and planning for a child.

It is important to emphasize that the strain reported in intimate relationships is not only due to changed daily routines, compounded by some degree of sleeplessness. Many couples report ruefully that what seems to suffer even more is the time and energy for the luxuries that nourish many adult intimate relationships: shared time reading together, going to films or museums, and relaxing together in a variety of ways that presume a childless existence. Furthermore, at least in the early years, a child is an interloper in the emotional and sexual aspects of a relationship as well. If you are spontaneous but private about your lovemaking, you may be sure that having to schedule it more carefully—working around your exhaustion and hoping the baby won't wake up—can have most discouraging effects. Although none of these disruptions need be permanent parts of parenthood, they can cause severe strains and losses for an initial period. The extent to which they become permanent family strains depends on how determined or conflicted each parent is about the priority of the new parent role versus the effort to continue developing and nourishing old roles.

One absolutely crucial dimension of potential change in your family roles is how you see yourself and your partner sharing the parental role if there is to be one. As noted earlier, traditionally, the parental role has components that are more or less mutually exclusive for each sex. In this model, male parents provide material resources for the family, and female parents provide for the details of maintenance and training, in addition to being the emotional, nurturing resource. This traditional division of parenting tasks can work cooperatively, but it can also create an atmosphere of competition and envy. At worst, the mother gives up the freedom of her own preparent life and of adult companionship with her mate and friends, and the father is excluded from the nurturing warmth of family relationships and from such feelings in himself. Children can thus become the focus of competition for their loyalty.

Many of us who grew up in families that functioned in this way to some extent would not choose to repeat that experience. We may recall fathers who were successful in their careers but rarely available and mothers who admitted that they would have chosen a different life pattern if a choice had been available. In Patricia Brooks's study of families of corporate executives, among the male children of college age, fewer than one-fifth were planning career paths similar to those of their fathers.[12] The majority stated that they did not want to have jobs in which they would be separated from human values and enduring relationships or would have to be away from home a great deal. This was a rejection not only of the time demands of such a career, but also of traditional masculine values of aggressive competitiveness and denial of the emotional aspects of relationships. In a similar vein, a study by the Human Resources Department at American Telephone and Telegraph found that younger managers in ten major industries were less interested than their seniors in getting ahead; they also stated that they cared less about the organization than about their families.[13] The conclusion of Douglas Bray, the research director, is that the new family focus on fatherhood is reducing the motivation of U.S. business managers to succeed at all costs. This study found no difference in the abilities of the younger managers—just in their priorities. Unlike the beginning executives of a generation ago, the current crop was much more likely to be involved in child care arrangements and other parenting tasks that encroached on work expectations. Furthermore, the younger managers, besides participating more in family life, showed increased motivation to receive and give sympathy and help to fellow workers, rather than competing with them as in the past.

Men may want to be more involved in the caring, nurturing aspects of life, and women may agree that this change would be beneficial, but lack of experience, lack of suitable role models, and not-so-subtle social pressures may make such changes difficult. There are sound reasons why work and family have been kept separate in this society. Many working women realize their own version of the lack of fit between the two roles as they have come to participate in the traditionally male provider role. This participation brings financial and psychological rewards for them, but they express concern about the lack of internal congruence between the assertive, competitive aspects of their adult working role and the softer, nurturing, necessarily more patient aspects of the traditional maternal role. It's not easy—for men or for women—to come home from a high-pressure work day and change roles completely to become gentle, receptive, and nurturing. The infamous after-work cocktail helps many make the transition.

It should be clear by now that consideration of the parenthood choice within a social context forces you to assess the balance between your working role and your family role and the extent (or lack) of fit between these roles as they are and as you would like them to be. Most people can and do live with some discrepancies between the ideal and the reality, because there is an inherent conflict between roles that are completely devoted to work and those that are completely devoted to family life.

A *Wall Street Journal* survey reports that chief executive officers of the 1,300 largest corporations typically work sixty to seventy hours a week, travel six to ten days a month, and give up their weekends for business meetings. "On the way to the top most relocated six or more times . . . most believe that a successful career requires personal sacrifices, and most put their jobs before their families or themselves."[14] In contrast, the *New York Times* describes Diane, the 40-year-old, college-educated wife of a successful executive in a large, midwestern corporation. Her own needs and happiness "come second to those of her husband and third and fourth to those of their two children."[15]

In a two-paycheck family, both partners can take more career chances and can explore alternatives more fully than either partner can in a single-paycheck family. However, many observers note that, in reality, the typical two-job family is really a three-job family; the man has a job and leisure time, while the woman has two jobs, at work and at home. A large study of couples in which both partners worked found that men experienced their nonwork time as leisure time for fun activities, whereas women reported their time spent off the job as more worklike, dealing with household tasks.[16] In short, says one author, women complain of fatigue and schedule conflicts, rather than complaining about men not doing their share or about employers continuing to operate as though every worker had a wife at home.[17] In *Family Politics*, Letty Pogrebin notes wryly that the female sex-role imperative has expanded to allow women to "have it all" as long as they can "do it all."[18] Since "having it all" has meant adding roles, not altering or renegotiating the demands of the existing ones, adding the role of parent may trigger "overload."

Regardless of the division of labor in family tasks, an intimate relationship should involve warmth, affection, respect, understanding, and support on both sides. Partners who are successful at maintaining intimacy in a childless situation sometimes find that parenting is the most formidable obstacle to the romance they still share. Some researchers of family life attribute the increased conflict that often accompanies parenting to the splitting of roles and tasks that are expected in traditional childrearing roles. Now that parenting styles and stereotyped sex-role behavior are being questioned, more partners are accepting childrearing as another family role to be shared. Philip Cowan, of the University of California at Berkeley, has found that fathers whose working hours permit them to be more involved with child care feel better about themselves, and their wives are less depressed, regardless of whether or not they are working mothers. He maintains that employers would do well to listen to what parents of either sex say they need as parents: "People shouldn't have to feel that they are sacrificing their best possible performance on their jobs in order to become parents."[19] As men see the positive aspects of developing their capacity for nurturing, and as women appreciate the benefits of creative and satisfying employment, the advantages of shared, inter-dependent parenting become more apparent. When two people are inter-dependent, it is not easy to balance demands and schedules and to agree on plans and tactics, but those who try agree that the benefits can be enormous. There have always been women who worked and were parents; the change is that more men now want to and can do both as well, to the benefit of all concerned.

There does tend to be more enthusiasm for sharing of family work (and rewards) among women than among men, whether or not parenting is included as part of that family work. Usually, people who live together have already worked out some arrangements for taking care of the necessary details of daily living; our concern here is to consider how these existing arrangements might be affected by a change in parenthood status. Not all families regard men's family work as limited to taking out the garbage; if all adults in a family work outside the home, and if family work is shared equally, the added demands of parenting work might also be divided. Those with experience, however, say not to count on it. Most men who have no parenting experience regard the early stages of parenting as something quite foreign to them but for which women have a natural instinct, or at least more familiarity; they have much cultural support for this view. In this day and age, neither the instinct argument nor the experience argument has much factual support, but they are still reinforced by long tradition. It is more likely that neither partner will have had much experience in the details of parenting. The truth is that the practice of parenting—like the practice of executive management, medicine, or gourmet cooking—can be learned by anyone with motivation, intelligence, and practice, regardless of any "gender handicap" at the start of the course. The issue is not potential capacity for the job, but whether or not you want the job enough to learn to do it well.

Friendship Roles

The role of friend is one that tends to be taken very much for granted by those who have some friends. If you have lost a close friend, however, or if you had had to leave some friends because of relocation, you may have considered the value of friendships in your life. Friends share our good and bad times; they also provide support, advice, a sympathetic ear, and often tangible help when it is needed. Most of us don't have enough time to spend with our friends as it is, even if we are childless. Curiously, the parenthood decisions can affect friendships no matter which decision is made.

Many childless people over 30 have already experienced the change in friendships that can occur when some friends become parents. As the one without a child, you may have seen your friends who have children change into people with less time, less energy, and fewer resources, but not necessarily less inclination for the friendship activities you shared. Their time is taken up with new tasks that are related to parenthood; at worst, their parenthood seems to be their only topic of conversation. It's rather like friends who move to a new city or a new job; they are full of descriptions and experiences that cannot be shared in the same ways as before. This need not be fatal to a friendship, but it often is. From the other side, consider how you as a permanently childless friend or a new-parent friend would relate to your existing friends. If the friendships that you value most do not depend on your work or on where you live, they are less likely to be changed by our parenthood choice. However, many professional women say that they feel they have betrayed childless friends of long standing when and if they choose parenthood. At present, there is no similar transition for men who become parents (although there is one when they settle down with a partner), but this may change with the new parenting roles fathers are choosing. Both the time and the opportunity to continue friendship activities with an old circle of friends diminish when people become parents. However, newly established parents, like newly established partners, can and do find similar people with whom they can establish new friendships; in the case of parenthood, this new social support may be even more valuable than the supports available when life was more carefree.

Single Parenthood

If you are considering single parenthood, a realistic assessment of your friendship, work, and family roles is even more important in facing your decision. Personal experience and discussions with many single parents of both sexes have convinced me that the single parenthood experience is not so much different as it is much more difficult than a partner parenthood situation. Being a single parent is very tough, primarily because you have to juggle all the role demands necessary for your personal survival and still take responsibility for all parenting tasks. For every single parent I know, the implacable monster is time; there are never enough hours in a day, and there is no time off. Most roles are easier to perform if there is some flexibility in them, but the single parent often finds that the extra time for activities such as exploring alternative work situations, finding a new child care resource, or caring for a sick child is just not there. This is important, because research on the effects of a single-parent environment on the health and development of children indicates that having a good relationship with one adult is sufficient for a child, provided that the adult is functioning reasonably well.[20] Also, it apparently is not so damaging for a child to be raised in a single-parent home as to grow up in a home with two adults who are in continual strife.

Children who are raised in single-parent households are also less likely to hold sex-linked stereotypes for adult behavior, simply because the parent who is present will be demonstrating both mothering and fathering. In such single-parent situations, however, the role of friends is even more crucial. For the parent, they can provide both nurturing and social support; for the child, they can provide the alternative adult role models that are essential for normal development. The most successful single parents I know have strong friendship networks that are a mix of old friends, who provide continuity for things that were valued before parenthood, and new ones, who provide help and support for parenting demands and challenges.

Summary: Assessing Your Social Context

Up to this point, we have discussed the various roles you currently fill as part of your daily life and how each role might change in the face of a decision about parenthood. This review might have seemed rather artificial, since you have been asked to imagine and predict changes that are only partially within your direct experience. More important, however, although it has been useful to assess each type of role separately, in reality they are interactive in ways that are crucial to your understanding of who you are now and who you may wish to become. Now it is time to assess your situation in its entirety, considering not just the pluses and minuses associated with each role but also their net sum in relation to a personal decision about parenthood.

Table 4–1 is a highly concentrated combination of the issues we have discussed into a summary assessment. This review process has some underlying assumptions. First, your daily life is assumed to be quite busy, even if you would not define the mix of activities as ideal. The decision process assumes, further, that something will have to change or give, but that you want to continue to meet what you have defined as your important needs.

Exercise 4 provides an outline within which you can assess your current social context. In the first three parts, assess your roles as worker, partner, and friend (and other roles) with regard to the rewards, demands, and potential compatibility of each with a parenthood role. For each role, list the details of your situation. If some aspects are much more important to you than others, you can underline them, or rank them, or use any other weighting system that is clear to you. For example, if I were completing the first part about my work role, I would note that my rewards come equally from teaching and research, but that I receive a low academic salary and minimal social support from my male colleagues. My assessment of the demand level is that it is very high, with long hours and expectations of productivity that require evening and weekend work, even though some of it can be done at home. Incompatibility problems would be likely to be serious, occur-

Table 4–1
Summary Assessment of Your Social Context

Your Major Roles	Rewards	Demands	Compatibility	Costs of Change
Worker	Do you consider your work a career? How important are the rewards provided: income? prestige? social support?	How rigid are the boundaries: location? hours? How much extra time is expected of you?	What areas of incompatibility do you predict between this role and a parent or nonparent role for you?	How much of this role would you be willing or able to give up: part-time? full-time? For how long?
Intimate partner	What are the rewards for you in this relationship?	What are your partner's expectations? How much time and energy do you give to the relationship?	How compatible is this role likely to be with a parent or a nonparent role?	How much of this relationship would you be able to give up? For how long?
Friend (and other important roles)	What are the rewards for you in these roles? How important are they to you?	What are others' expectations of you? How much of your time and energy do they take?	How compatible are these roles with the potential role of parent or nonparent?	Would you be willing and able to give up these roles? For how long?
Summary assessment range	Rewards very high, life is complete	Demands are high, all energy taken	Serious incompatibility with other role	Unable or unwilling to give up any
	· · ·	· · ·	· · ·	
	Rewards not enough	Demands OK some energy left	Compatibility is negotiable	Could give up all or some

Exercise 4
Assessing Your Social Context

A. Your Role as Worker

	Most Important	Less Important

Rewards
Do you consider your work
a career?

How important are the rewards
provided:
    Income?
    Prestige?
    Social support?

Demands
How rigid are the boundaries:
    Location?
    Hours?

How much extra time is
expected of you?

Compatibility
What areas of incompatibility
do you predict between this role
and a parent or nonparent role
for you?

Costs of Change
How much of this role would
you be willing or able to give
up:
    Part-time?
    Full-time?
    For how long?

B. Your Role as Intimate Partner

Rewards
What are the rewards for you in
this relationship?

Demands
What are your partner's
expectations?

How much time and energy do
you give to the relationship?

Compatibility
How compatible is this role
likely to be with a parent or
nonparent role?

Costs of Change
How much of this relationship
would you be able or willing to
give up? For how long?

Exercise 4 continued

	Most Important	Less Important
C. Your Role as Friend (and Other Important Roles)		

Rewards
What are the rewards for you in
these other relationships?

How important are they to
you?

Demands
What are others' expectations of
you?

How much of your time and
energy do they take?

Compatibility
How compatible are these roles
with the potential role of parent
or nonparent?

Costs of Change
Would you be able and willing
to put these roles on hold or
give them up? For how long?

D. Summary Assessment

1. When I consider the *rewards* of the social roles that are presently part of my life:

The rewards are very high; life feels rich and full.	The rewards are not enough for me.

2. When I assess the *demands* that come with my current roles as worker, lover, and friend:

They seem high, and most or all of my available energy is taken.	They seem to be manageable; some energy is available.

3. When I consider the potential *compatibility* of my present roles with the potential role of parent or nonparent:

I can predict some serious incompatibility problems.	Compatibility is negotiable.

4. When I consider the potential *costs of change* in my present roles that might come with the new role:

I feel unable or unwilling to give up what I have now.	I could give up some or all of some present roles.

ring both at the practical level, because of time conflicts, but also at the personal level, because my colleagues would judge my parenthood as evidence of less than a full commitment to my professional career. I would not want to give up my career completely, but I have often considered cutting back to part-time if that could be arranged.

When you have made a similar appraisal of each of your roles, build a summary of your present social situation in the final section of the exercise by grouping the rewards for each role, then the demands for each one, and so forth. In the summary, consider, first, the rewards associated with all of the roles we have discussed. The exercise provides a range of possible responses that can describe your net status with regard to the rewards in your life at present—ranging from your feeling that the rewards from your current roles are very high to your belief that the available rewards are inadequate, for any number of reasons. Similarly, combine your assessment of the net demands of your various roles and describe your current situation with regard to your supply of energy to meet these demands. Your consideration of potential incompatibilities between role expectations follows your review of their demands because the costs of resolving very incompatible roles include the expenditure of extra energy that you may or may not have to give. Finally, consider the potentially most severe cost of change—giving up a role you now hold, even if only partially or temporarily.

Each of these summary assessments has implications for a decision about parenthood; although they are related to one another, they can vary widely for each person. To the extent that your personal assessment is near the top of each summary range, the logistical aspects of a choice for parenthood may be especially difficult for you. For example, if you describe your current situation as one in which the rewards are high, and if these roles take all of your time and energy, but you would not want to give up or change any of them, then a choice for parenthood at this time could cause serious problems in your daily life. If your assessments fall more toward the lower end of the assessment range, however, there is at least room for you to consider changes that might come whether you decide for or against parenthood.

It may sound at this point as though the only decision point is whether you can fit a child into the pace and pattern of your life. That has been the decision issue addressed in this chapter, but it is important to remember that this environmental focus is only part of the larger context of decision making about parenthood. If you are wrestling with other parts of that decision as primary issues, this logistical assessment perspective can only contribute some of the information that may be useful to you in understanding why the decision issues are difficult for you. If you are concerned more with feasibility issues around parenthood, this summary assessment will be directly relevant to your primary concerns.

Many of you may be uncertain where you fit in these descriptions. If you are thinking, "All this is somewhat relevant, but it does not really address how I feel about parenthood or whether I really want to make a permanent choice," then the discussion in the next chapter is important for you. The up-to-date information presented so far can help you separate fact from fiction regarding the medical and logistical aspects of the parenthood decision, as well as providing insights from the experience of others. Nonetheless, there is a more personal, introspective dimension of the parenthood decision that is equally essential but is relatively independent of the facts already presented. Now that you know so much about parenthood, it's time to see how you *feel* about the prospect.

Notes

1. A. Coleman and L. Coleman, *Earth Father/Sky Father: The Changing Concept of Fathering* (Englewood Cliffs, N.J.: Prentice-Hall, 1981).

2. *San Francisco Chronicle,* April 30, 1984.

3. C. Bird, *The Two Paycheck Marriage* (New York: Rawson, Wade, 1979).

4. L. Bodine, "Sandra Day O'Connor," *American Bar Association Journal* 69(1983):1397.

5. A study by J. Simmons of the University of Michigan, described in G. Norris and J. Miller, *The Working Mother's Complete Handbook* (New York: Dutton, 1979).

6. M. Fabe and N. Wikler, *Up Against the Clock: Career Women Speak on the Choice to Have Children* (New York: Random House, 1979), pp. 46–47.

7. M.C. Howell, "Employed Mothers and Their Families: A Review of Research," *Pediatrics* 52(1978):252–270.

8. A. Shreve, "Working Women as Role Models," *New York Times Sunday Magazine,* September 8, 1984.

9. L.W. Hoffman and F.I. Nye, *Working Mothers: An Evaluative Review of the Consequences for Wife, Husband, and Child* (San Francisco: Jossey-Bass, 1974).

10. Roper 1980 National Opinion Poll, described in L.C. Pogrebin, *Family Politics: Love and Power on an Intimate Frontier* (New York: McGraw-Hill, 1983).

11. A study of the effects of first parenthood, by E.E. LeMasters, described in E. Peck and W. Granzig, *The Parent Test* (New York: Putnam, 1978).

12. P. Brooks, "Whatever Happened to Following in Dad's Footsteps?" *TWA Ambassador,* May 1977, pp. 18–22.

13. D. Bray, Contribution to a panel discussion, "Changing Patterns of Work and Family Roles," at the Annual Meeting of the American Psychological Association, Anaheim, Calif., August 1982.

14. *Wall Street Journal,* August 19, 1980.

15. *New York Times,* March 11, 1979.

16. J. Pleck, "The Work–Family Problem: Overloading the System," in B. Forisha and B. Goldsmith (eds.), *Women and Organizations: Outsiders on the Inside* (Englewood Cliffs, N.J.: Prentice-Hall, 1981), pp. 239–254.

17. P. Daniels and K. Weingarten, *Sooner or Later: The Timing of Parenthood in Adult Lives* (New York: Norton, 1982). These authors note that for "late timing" couples, the parenthood crisis and overload is more a case of making room in an

already complex schedule, in which management and care issues are often already more clearly defined than they are for couples who begin parenthood at younger ages.

18. Pogrebin, *Family Politics*.

19. P. Cowan, Contribution to a panel discussion, "Changing Patterns of Work and Family," at the Annual Meeting of the American Psychological Association, Anaheim, Calif., August 1982.

20. Norris and Miller, *The Working Mother's Complete Handbook*. See also S.L. Atlas, *Single Parenting* (Englewood Cliffs, N.J.: Prentice-Hall, 1981).

5
Making a Personal Choice

This chapter discusses your feelings as you face the relatively unique combination of circumstances involved in making a major decision about parenthood. After all, you are considering taking on a major responsibility under conditions of near-maximum uncertainty and unpredictability. By the time they reach their thirties, most people have made some major decisions, such as taking a new position or purchasing a home. Although such responsibility-laden decisions carry some emotional freight and include some elements of the unknown, the anxiety they cause is diminished somewhat by the knowledge that you have obtained and used relevant information about the decision and that if you are not satisfied with your choice in the future, you can change your mind—you can seek another job or sell the house. The parenthood choice is different. A child cannot be returned or exchanged, and even if you have gathered extensive information, you cannot be sure how a child will turn out or how well you will function as a parent.

This chapter will help you assess how you feel about this most uncertain of choices. We will begin by assessing your personal circumstances, just as we began in the last chapter by assessing your environmental circumstances. Just as there was no "ideal" set of environmental circumstances that made certain a specific choice about parenthood, no combination of personal characteristics guarantees a correct parenthood choice. However, comparison of your personal description with the self-descriptions of others and their experiences may help you gain insights that may be useful to you in reaching a decision.

After assessing your personal characteristics, the next step will be to consider how satisfied you are with yourself and how you see yourself changing in the future. In part, this look into the future is necessary because the decision about parenthood does not affect just the next year or two. Childhood and adolescence do not go on forever, but some parents will swear that there are times when it seems that way. The other reason for assessing potential personal change is that there are some important reasons *not* to decide for parenthood, several of which involve hopes that having children will change your life in ways that you desire.

Finally, you will be asked to try on both of the identities that could follow a decision about parenthood. You will be asked to imagine yourself as a parent and as a permanently childfree person, both in the present and in the future. This exercise will be imaginary and full of unknowns, but what is important is not how well you can imagine but how you feel about each alternative. Emotional reactions are important predictors in their own right; whether you *feel* that something is challenging or threatening, exciting, boring, or terrifying can be independent of any facts involved. It is important to identify the specific nature of your emotional reactions to parenthood or nonparenthood, regardless of their source or their relationship to factual circumstances. Why you react as you do may be difficult and time-consuming to understand and is generally beyond the scope of this book. Especially if your feelings are very troubling to you or your partner, you may well require the services of a professional counselor who is experienced in family relationships. Ignoring disturbing feelings and going ahead with a decision about parenthood will not make the feelings disappear and may well create additional disturbances in other aspects of your life.

Describing Yourself as You Are Now

There are an infinite number of ways in which people can describe themselves. The rather small group of descriptive characteristics to be reviewed here were chosen because they have been mentioned in studies of people who were satisfied with their decision to remain childless or of people who were successful at and satisfied with parenthood. In Exercise 5, begin by considering each of the descriptive characteristics listed, and decide which of them describe you as you are now, not as you might like to be or believe that you should be.

The first three characteristics involve your sense of your independence, flexibility, and growth. Your choice of a self-rating statement also reflects how important these personal characteristics are to you. These three characteristics have been grouped together because they often figure prominently in the self-descriptions of people who have chosen to remain childless and who have expressed satisfaction with that choice; that is, people who have rated themselves high on these characteristics and consider them very important parts of their core identity tend to see the costs and responsibilities of parenthood as outweighing the potential rewards of that status. Research comparing the voluntarily childfree with parents of the same age and socioeconomic level indicates that the former are equally as interested in others and are no more interested in material gains than their parent counterparts—nor do they differ in level of maturity, self-esteem, or life satisfaction. Veevers, who has done a great deal of research on the childless, identifies the crucial distin-

Exercise 5
Describing Yourself as You Are Now

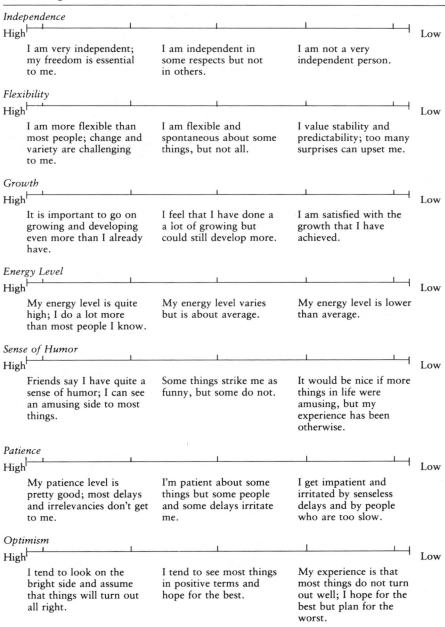

Independence

High |————————————————————————————————| Low

I am very independent;
my freedom is essential
to me.

I am independent in
some respects but not
in others.

I am not a very
independent person.

Flexibility

High |————————————————————————————————| Low

I am more flexible than
most people; change and
variety are challenging
to me.

I am flexible and
spontaneous about some
things, but not all.

I value stability and
predictability; too many
surprises can upset me.

Growth

High |————————————————————————————————| Low

It is important to go on
growing and developing
even more than I already
have.

I feel that I have done a
a lot of growing but
could still develop more.

I am satisfied with the
growth that I have
achieved.

Energy Level

High |————————————————————————————————| Low

My energy level is quite
high; I do a lot more
than most people I know.

My energy level varies
but is about average.

My energy level is lower
than average.

Sense of Humor

High |————————————————————————————————| Low

Friends say I have quite a
sense of humor; I can see
an amusing side to most
things.

Some things strike me as
funny, but some do not.

It would be nice if more
things in life were
amusing, but my
experience has been
otherwise.

Patience

High |————————————————————————————————| Low

My patience level is
pretty good; most delays
and irrelevancies don't get
to me.

I'm patient about some
things but some people
and some delays irritate
me.

I get impatient and
irritated by senseless
delays and by people
who are too slow.

Optimism

High |————————————————————————————————| Low

I tend to look on the
bright side and assume
that things will turn out
all right.

I tend to see most things
in positive terms and
hope for the best.

My experience is that
most things do not turn
out well; I hope for the
best but plan for the
worst.

Exercise 5 (continued)

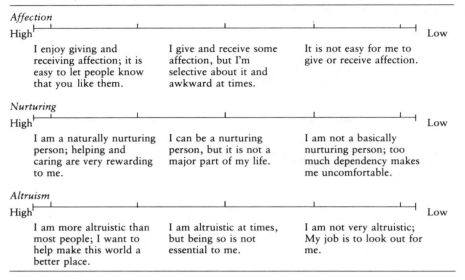

Affection

High ⊢——————————————————————————⊣ Low

I enjoy giving and receiving affection; it is easy to let people know that you like them.	I give and receive some affection, but I'm selective about it and awkward at times.	It is not easy for me to give or receive affection.

Nurturing

High ⊢——————————————————————————⊣ Low

I am a naturally nurturing person; helping and caring are very rewarding to me.	I can be a nurturing person, but it is not a major part of my life.	I am not a basically nurturing person; too much dependency makes me uncomfortable.

Altruism

High ⊢——————————————————————————⊣ Low

I am more altruistic than most people; I want to help make this world a better place.	I am altruistic at times, but being so is not essential to me.	I am not very altruistic; My job is to look out for me.

guishing characteristic as what she calls a "purposeful wanderlust"—not just yearning but saving for and planning a life with personal achievement, adventure, and novelty. The childfree emphasize new experiences, new places, new goals, and personal challenges in their lives.[1]

It is important to point out that these three characteristics are the only ones among those presented here that have distinguished the childfree from their peers. They may describe themselves as high or low on the other personal characteristics listed, and their patterns of self-description in terms of patience, energy level, sense of humor, and the like, do not differ from those who are parents or are still undecided.[2] If you found yourself expecting otherwise, you have not just heard but have partially accepted the negative stereotypes about people who choose to remain childless. They are not really more selfish, immature, pessimistic, or unloving, on the average, than other people. Perhaps as more people take care in reaching a decision about parenthood, these myths will diminish in strength.

It may also have occurred to you that there is a sex-role dimension to this discussion, just as there was in the preceding chapter. Although the person who lives for challenge, adventure, achievement, and growth has more often been male than female in our cultural tradition, this pattern is neither necessary nor inevitable. Each of the characteristics discussed in this chapter can describe both men and women. You may feel that a person of the same sex should score differently than your self-ratings on some of these characteristics; if you do, that belief should be considered as part of your self-assessment in the next section of this chapter.

The next four characteristics in the exercise (energy level, sense of humor, patience, optimism) are not essential to either side of the parenthood choice. However, high levels of these characteristics will surely help if you do choose parenthood. Studies of successful parents have found that mothers and fathers who are satisfied with their parenting and are rated as successful by their children and others tend to report that they are at the high end in each of these descriptions.[3] For example, a high energy level helps parents because, as Erma Bombeck points out, parenthood means that you will never have uninterrupted sleep again. If you think that only infants keep you up, she cautions, wait until they are teenagers and you sit waiting by the phone for the police to call because it is 3:00 A.M. and they're out with the family car.[4] Patience involves not only a tolerance for endless, repeated questions and dawdling of unheard-of duration but also the ability to defer your own personal gratifications—for example, postponing going out to dinner and a show until the children have finished college. Furthermore, children are either too rational or too nonrational to succumb to parental wiles; either can be frustrating. For example, there is a cartoon showing a father emerging from an infant's room and saying: "She is going to have everything in the world, all the advantages we can provide. She can go to the college of her choice. So why is she crying?"[5] If these vignettes of parenthood make you smile, your sense of humor about the exigencies of parenthood is apparently in good shape.

The final three personal characteristics in the exercise are affection, nurturing, and altruism. People who score high on these characteristics are clearly more oriented to the interpersonal relationships in their lives, whether or not these include parenthood. They are included in this discussion because they describe some central characteristics of people who have been found to be successful parents. A positive nurturing attitude, a genuine liking for children, and personal gratification from giving help and affection described the successful parents in one major research study. Although fewer than 20 percent of the parents in that study were over 25 when they had their first child, the "older" subgroup comprised a very high proportion of the parents who were found to be successful; more than 80 percent of the successful parents had waited until they were older to begin parenthood.[6]

Be sure, again, that you are not making gender assumptions here. These successful parenting characteristics are not only feminine. One of the most successful single parents I know shared custody of his children half-time. His affection was more likely to take the form of friendly thumps and bumps than cuddling, but his children recognized the genuine article, and they thrived on his care and regard for them.

Self-Acceptance and Motivation for Change

Now it is time to assess your satisfaction with your current state. You may have looked at your self-ratings in Exercise 5 and been satisfied with the mix of personal characteristics you chose to describe yourself at present. If so, congratulations; the ability to know and accept yourself as you are is not granted to many.

Some degree of dissatisfaction is much more typical, however. In general, this dissatisfaction takes one of two forms: you feel that you may really be different from your current self-description, but you have not had the opportunity to discover whether this is so; or you would like to be more (or less) affectionate, or flexible, or energetic, because you believe it is a better way for people to be. The former reasoning implies more satisfaction with what you are and sees possible changes in terms of the opportunity to experience them; the latter implies dissatisfaction with some aspects of yourself and sees changes as things that *should* be or that others would like you to be.

Some examples may help clarify the differences between these two influences toward personal change. Suppose that you have described yourself as near the middle on the independence characteristic. The positive, exploring impetus for change might be expressed by a statement such as, "I've been pretty successful on my own for some time, but the time has come when I feel more like settling down and putting down some roots." In contrast, statements that imply change-as-obligation might sound more like "I've been pretty footloose, but my parents really want me to settle down now" or "My partner thinks that I'm too dependent as it is." People do change their personal characteristics, but the process is neither rapid nor easy. Clearly, changes that you feel are positive and self-chosen are more likely to occur and succeed than those that are attempted because you feel that you should. If some of the personal pressures regarding your parenthood decision appear to be the latter kind, they are demonstrably poor bases for deciding such an important issue affecting your future.

To assess your self-acceptance and motivation for change, consider your personal future—how you would describe yourself if your present plans and dreams were realized. What sort of person do you want to be five, ten, or twenty years from now? We all sense some changes that come with increased maturity; I am certainly a different person now, in many ways, than I was at 20 or at 30. I like to think that I am more the kind of person that I wanted to be even then, but maturity and growth have come slowly for me, with some wrong turns along the way. The view that I now have of myself is consistent with parenthood, but it was not always so—and my personal image does not necessarily include parenthood. I think I could be complete and happy with other ways of satisfying my own strong needs to nurture.

What do you want to become with the time you have in the future? Part of my personal definition of my future is that I have an obligation to accomplish some worthwhile things during my time here, in the sense that the world should be at least no worse off and, if possible, somewhat better for the time I have spent in it. For each of us, the question should be whether that future time includes, or at least is not in conflict with, the time necessary to be a good parent.

How does all this self-assessment apply to making a decision about parenthood? At the most basic level, it is always useful to take both personal and environmental circumstances into account when facing any major decision. You are considering here whether you have the personal characteristics that you think are relevant to either parenthood choice and also how comfortable you are with these characteristics. Following through with a decision to become a parent or to remain childless will surely change you to some degree, but these changes are likely to involve developing stronger levels or tapping deeper resources of the characteristics you already have, rather than developing new ones. Either choice is much less likely to change you in ways that you or others think you should change.

Adding Nonparent or Parent to Who You Are Now

However you may see yourself at present, it is now time to try on, at least in fantasy, the additions of you-as-nonparent and you-as-parent. The point of these exercises in imagination is not to see how accurate, detailed, or complete these potential identities may be, but to monitor your most basic emotional reactions to each of them. Insofar as you can, keep an open mind about seeing yourself as either parent or nonparent. This will not be so easy as you may think, because we have all been exposed to assumptions and stereotypes about the sorts of people who are and are not parents.

Imagining Yourself as Permanently Childless

People who have chosen to be permanently childfree often do not say so publicly because of the social disapproval they have found to be attached to that status. In teaching seminars on facing the decision about parenthood after 30, I have found that it is much more difficult to find guest speakers who admit that their choice to be childless is permanent than it is to find people who are positive about later parenthood or even single parents. People who have chosen to be childfree see themselves as having freedom, flexibility, and spontaneity in their lives. Many of them (but not all) like children, and they are often employed in demanding social service settings and in teaching the young. They may also describe themselves as favorite aunts and uncles, free to share special occasions and confidences with children without, as one person described it, the "moral obligation trips" of parenthood. Yet all of these people have experienced the more or less subtle pressures of pronatalism, which imply that they are immature, irresponsible, cold, and selfish because they do not choose to have children. Especially if they are married, they say it is easier to let people think that they cannot have children than to admit that they have chosen not to. As one person told me: "At least then they quit hassling you about it."

For women, the "motherhood myth" classifies them in a deviant position if they identify themselves as childless by choice. As Betty Rollin defines it, the myth is that having babies is something all "normal" women instinctively want and need and will enjoy doing. She points out:

> One of the more absurd aspects of the motherhood myth is the underlying assumption that, since women are biologically equipped to bear children, they are mentally, psychologically, emotionally, and technically equipped to rear them. To assume that such an exacting, consuming, and important task is something all women are equipped to do is far more dangerous and ridiculous than assuming that everyone with vocal chords should seek a career in opera.[7]

I asked a woman in her late thirties—who appeared to me to have all of the warm, nurturing, sensitive personal qualities that I felt would be ideal for parenthood—how she came to see herself as permanently childless. I knew that she genuinely liked children; I had observed her ability to relate to them at their own levels, so that even shy children warmed to her attention and interest in them. In response to my question, she laughed and said that it had begun early, because she had no illusions about parenting. Although she was the youngest of three children, she had helped raise her older brother's family of ten, and she felt that even three parents were insufficient. As she grew through her professional education and training, she came to realize that, for her, stability in her intimate relationships and quiet privacy were essential for giving her the energy and focus for maintaining the ability to draw out and understand people that her work required.

A man in his early forties related that he sometimes thought about having children of his own but that he came from a family of eight and knew first-hand the complications children bring to one's life. He spends frequent weekend days visiting his siblings and their assorted broods, and he enjoys extended solo outings with older nephews and nieces. His career as a trial lawyer is very demanding, requiring frequent trips out of town to represent clients. He also has a long-standing and mutually nurturing relationship with a professional woman who has a similarly demanding schedule. At some point in his thirties, he came to the conclusion that a childless life made the most sense for him. Although he enjoys being an uncle on occasion, he says that he never really thinks of himself as a potential father.

Another man spoke to me painfully of his deep sense that he could never be able to "father" effectively. He remembered his own father as one who was seldom at home; when he was present, he was distant from or negative toward his children. This man's father lived the "breadwinner" role and expected his wife "to take care of the children and present them for inspection occasionally." Thus, the man remembers time with his father as judgmental, rather than supportive. This man was sensitive to the changing expectations for the male role in parenting held by women he knew, and he was certain that he would be unable to meet these new expectations.

A woman whose career was in nursing said that she still thought occasionally of having children of her own but that such thoughts were rarely strong enough to make her question her discovery, several years earlier, that she and her husband had tacitly agreed that, for them, starting a family in their mid-thirties was just not feasible. She said that her husband had left the decision pretty much up to her. Once she faced it, she said, she realized that she felt no need to be a mother:

> I do a lot of mothering in my work, and especially now that I've been working with cancer patients, I come home some nights and I'm nearly burned out emotionally. The care I give is important to me—in a way, my patients are my children. To come home to my own, well, I would worry that they would deserve more from me than I could give them at times like that.

To assess how *you* feel about being childless permanently, consider the following situations:

1. Imagine that you have just discovered that you or your partner is definitely unable to have children. What are your feelings about this news?
2. Imagine yourself telling your partner, friends, co-workers, and family that you have reached a decision to be childfree permanently. Imagine, further, that they will be upset by your news. How will their reactions make you feel?
3. Imagine that a co-worker or friend, much like yourself but five or ten years younger, comes to you with his or her concern about making the parenthood decision. How would you present your decision to remain childless and your reactions to him or her?
4. Imagine yourself at age 50 and at age 65. What sort of person do you think you will be then if you are leading the childfree life you imagine? Although the most obvious concern is possible loneliness, remember that the loneliest people are those who presumed that their children would forestall a lonely future and who have been disappointed in that hope.

When you have worked through these questions, you will have reached some sense of your feelings about yourself as a potentially childless person, both now and in the future. One common reaction is a sense of loss and grieving for what might have been, which may or may not be mixed with a sense of relief and release. Take note, also, of the intensity of your feelings; their strength is also relevant to the personal decision process to come.

Imagining Yourself as a Parent

Now it is time to consider the other side of the coin. As you imagined the possible identity of a permanent childless person, imagine yourself as inclined toward parenthood, and assess your feelings and their intensity in response to the following situations:

1. Imagine that you have just discovered that you are pregnant (or your partner is). What is your emotional reaction to this news? You may already have had this experience in the past; if so, consider, also, whether your reaction now would be the same as it was then.
2. Imagine yourself as the parent of an infant or toddler a year or two from now. Suppose, further, that yours is the type of child who strains both physical and emotional resources—one who is oversensitive, wails a lot, and sleeps much less than you have been led to believe is usual. What are your parental feelings in this situation?
3. Now imagine yourself with a child of 8 or 10; you will be ten years older than you are now. How will you, as a parent, feel about constant disasters in the kitchen or repeated trips to the emergency room for broken bones and stitches? How will you feel if your child is reported to have problems in school or is caught stealing something from a store?
4. Imagine yourself as the parent of a difficult adolescent. (Some parents would retort: "Is there any other kind?") By now, of course, you will be five or ten years older still. How will you feel as a parent by that stage?

Each of these situations is in the middle range of parental experience. You could imagine a bright, loving, parental situation, in which everything goes well, or one that includes really serious disasters, such as major birth defects or behavioral problems; if the details of the situation determine your emotional reaction, however, you may conclude that you are still tentative about parenthood as a personal identity for you.

Both an obstetrician in private practice and a woman who worked in a Planned Parenthood clinic where many pregnancy tests were performed have told me that a surprising number of clients react to the confirmation of pregnancy with shock and denial—even though they have come in for testing because of prolonged and fairly unambiguous symptoms of early pregnancy. The emotional reaction that follows close upon the news can vary tremendously, from thrilled and euphoric to terrified. In *Letter to a Child Never*

Born, Oriana Fallaci provides an intense description of her emotional reaction to discovering her pregnancy:

> You existed. It was as if a bullet had struck me. My heart stopped. And when it began to pound again, it was in gun bursts of wonder. I had the feeling that everything was unsure and terrifying. Now I am locked in fear that soaks my face, my hair, my thoughts. I am lost in it. It is not fear of others. I don't care about others. It's not fear of God. I don't believe in God. It's not fear of pain. I have no fear of pain. It is fear of you, of the circumstance that has wrenched you out of nothingness to attach yourself to my body.[8]

For many people, the confirmation of pregnancy is the point at which their awareness of the enormity and uncertainty of parenthood begins. A certain amount of trepidation and ambivalence is to be expected for those who are most positively inclined toward parenthood. Even with a healthy respect for the unknowable, some potential parents report that their emotional state at this point includes a calm center amidst the excitement and turmoil, a sense of readiness and acceptance of the identity of parent, even if the process has a long way to go. One woman who described herself to me as an unlikely mother (at 35, she was single, had a precarious financial status, and was very active politically), said that her readiness for parenthood had little to do with the facts of her situation. She gave the same description of her readiness as is given by many whose circumstances are more favorable: she was ready for a deeper commitment that would give more meaning to her life. Although the decision was scary and risky, it was also personally satisfying and rewarding for her.

In her sensitive portrayal of aging, *Coming of Age,* Simone de Beauvoir writes:

> The warmest and happiest feelings that old people experience are those that have to do with their grandchildren. . . . The friendship of the young is very valuable to old people, quite apart from any family tie; it gives them the feeling that these times in which they are living are still their own times; it revives their own youth; it carries them along the infinity of the future and it is the best defense against the gloom that threatens old age. Unfortunately, relations of this sort are rare, for the young and the old belong to two worlds between which there is little communication.[9]

When you imagine how you might feel as the parent of an older child or an adolescent, the experiences of your own parents can be a major influence on your imagery. Several examples were presented earlier of people whose uncertainty and ambivalence about parenthood was based, at least in part, on their recollections of their parents' experience when they were growing up. If you had a parent who was unhappy, frustrated, or unfulfilled, you may well wonder how you will feel about the same situation, even if your life is very different and you have already achieved your development goals.

Norris and Miller present another emotional pitfall as if it were inherent among working parents. They say that everyone feels guilty; the only issues are (1) how reasonable your level of guilt is and (2) what it is making you do that is unproductive.[10] Other authors do not necessarily agree, however. Novelist Margaret Drabble, for example, notes that her attitudes and feelings about children changed drastically with the experience of parenthood. Before she became a parent, she was sure that, besides being expensive and either boring or irritating, children would also be a hindrance to her career. Now she reports that her children are her greatest pleasure, but she also notes that if she claimed this publicly, some people would assume that she was "simply being polite, dutiful, womanly, and deceitful."[11]

As you consider the possible identity of parent later in your own life cycle, the main issue may come to be a variation of a very old question— whether it is better to have loved and lost than never to have loved at all. This is not a reference to the inevitable slipping away that all parents experience sooner or later as their children grow into adult lives of their own. Rather, it refers to the experience of parenthood as a losing rather than a winning experience. In 1976, newspaper columnist Ann Landers, having received a letter asking the question, in turn asked her readers: "If you had to do it over again, would you have children?" She received more than 10,000 replies, of which an astounding 70 percent answered no. The reasons people gave were many, but the most common ones were that the state of the world had changed so much for the worse; that their children had grown up, despite their best efforts, to be neglectful, unlikable, or even criminal; and that the best years of their marriages had been the ones before children. A disproportionate number of responses were from single parents, who described their lives as difficult or impossible.[12] I received a similar response from a divorced mother, who said:

> I only wish that I had made sure that I had a really strong relationship before I had them. Every day now I know that I didn't do any of us a favor by having them. I feel sorry for my kids; they remind me constantly of the failure of my relationship with their father. I try to be both mother and father to them, but they and I know that I'm doing a bad job.

Of course, people who choose to respond to an inquiry like the one by Ann Landers may do so because they have strong feelings about the experience, and they may not be typical of all parents. The only nationally representative information of this question comes from two studies that were done ten years apart—the Princeton Roper Poll in 1965 and the Gallup Poll in 1975.[13] In the earlier poll, only 1 percent of the respondents said that they would not become parents again if they had the choice; ten years later, 10 percent answered negatively. The most logical conclusion is not that parenthood became so much worse during that decade, but that more honest answers to the question became increasingly acceptable in a social atmosphere that questioned pronatalism and advocated more freedom of choice about parenthood.

There have probably always been some parents who regretted having children when it was too late, and there will continue to be some in the future. The effort here is to try to identify circumstances that will allow some people to predict in advance that parenthood is an inappropriate choice for them. My ancestors were great believers in the old adage, "Hope for the best, but plan for the worst." Perhaps, finally, that is the best level of preparation that can be achieved. If your vision of parenthood includes only the rosiest images, the life you plan may have little relation to the life you will live.

Summary

As I have noted several times, your decision about parenthood will be, in the end, a very personal and at least somewhat emotional choice. This chapter has reviewed some of the dimensions of that emotional choice, taking into consideration who you are now and who you think you would like to be in the future. In light of this personal assessment and your feelings about it, you have been asked to consider yourself in the identity of a permanently childless person and in the identity of a parent. Most important, you have been urged to identify your emotional reactions to each of these possible identities. Now that you have done so, you may have discovered that you feel much more strongly about one identity than you do about the other, although these strong feelings may be either positive or negative. You may also be surprised to realize that your emotional reaction to either possibility is not as closely related to the facts of your situation as you might have expected; at least, that is often the case. Especially if you have found that your emotional reaction is much stronger than you had expected, take this reaction most seriously, and give it at least as much weight in the final decision process as you give the facts involved. That reaction taps an essential dimension of your future and your potential success in it that cannot be included in any other way.

Notes

1. J. Veevers, *Childless by Choice* (Toronto: Butterworth, 1980); R. Kramer "The No-Child Family," *New York Times Sunday Magazine*, December 24, 1972.

2. L. Silka and S. Kiesler, "Couples Who Choose to Remain Childless," *Family Planning Perspectives*, January 1977, pp. 7–9.

3. E. Peck and W. Granzig, *The Parent Test* (New York: Putnam, 1978), pp. 149–154.

4. Bombeck, E. *Motherhood: The Second Oldest Profession* (New York: McGraw-Hill, 1983).

5. Peck and Granzig, *The Parent Test,* p. 236.

6. Ibid., p. 66.

7. From "Motherhood: Who Needs It?" by Betty Rollin, *Look* Magazine, September 22, 1970. © 1970 by Cowles Broadcasting, Inc. Reprinted with permission.

8. O. Fallaci, *Letter to a Child Never Born* (New York: Simon and Schuster, 1976), p. 9.

9. S. de Beauvoir, *The Coming of Age* (New York: G.P. Putnam's Sons, 1972), pp. 474–475.

10. G. Norris and J. Miller, *The Working Mother's Complete Handbook* (New York: Plume, New American Library, 1984), pp. 231–238.

11. M. Drabble, "All My Love, Mama," *New York Times Sunday Magazine,* August 4, 1984.

12. A. Landers, "If You Had to Do It All Over Again, Would You Have Children?" *Good Housekeeping,* June 1976.

13. Polls described in E.M. Whelan, *A Baby? . . . Maybe* (Indianapolis and New York: Bobbs-Merrill, 1975), pp. 165–166.

6
Anticipating the Future for Each Choice

Review of Delaying Issues

This book began by describing the circumstances that have led to important changes in social patterns in this country. By accident or by design, a significant number of people have come to the point of facing the parenthood decision at a much later stage in their life cycles than has been traditional in our culture. On the average, people are marrying later—many not before age 30—and the pattern of marriage-then-parenthood is no longer taken for granted. Although there have always been some people who faced potential parenthood later in life, their experience was unusual, and they rarely had the benefit of learning from similar experiences of others or of the social support provided by sharing the experience. The basic purpose of this book, then, has been to share the decision experience with you, to give you the opportunity to learn from the experience of others and from relevant research findings. The components of the decision process (medical and genetic, career, social, and personal) have been presented separately so that you could consider each of them from your own decision-making perspective.

As a first step, you were asked to outline your own reasons for delay in reaching this point of decision. Basically, two aspects of the decision-delaying process are important. In positive terms, the delay included recognition of the time and resources available for furthering your personal development. For most people, the delay also included recognition of the value of finding and developing a secure, rewarding intimate relationship as a necessary prerequisite for consideration of possible parenthood. In other words, some people have delayed because they want the best possible conditions to exist before they consider facing the commitments of parenthood.

It is ironic that these concerns for the "right" circumstances have led many people to current situations that are now described in terms of risk rather than advantage. Those who have accomplished a great deal in their personal or career development and those who have achieved rich and rewarding intimate relationships now find themselves wondering what parenthood might cost them in terms of maintaining their present circumstances. The responsibilities and demands of parenthood are often more visible to them than its joys and rewards as they observe the experiences of their friends and co-workers who are parents.

Even those who honestly claim that they have never felt a deep personal need to be parents report some degree of uncertainty about the permanence of their present feelings as the biological clock continues to tick away. They wonder whether they will always feel as they do now and what they might miss if they choose a permanently childless status; after all, the majority of people do become parents sooner or later. Unlike those who are asking themselves whether this is the right time for parenthood, members of this small but growing group are asking themselves whether they should make a permanent commitment to a childfree life.

For all of these people, the risk associated with the passage of time comes into focus more and more prominently as they grow older. As a 40-year-old potential parent told me recently: "The nice thing about delay is that you don't have to live with the consequences of a decision, but now we're at the point where the delay is forcing our decision to the panic point." Certainly, a person who is 40 has more cause to be concerned about the passage of time than one who is 30. At any age, however, the issues of whether and why to choose parenthood provide a much sounder basis for a decision than the factor of age, which has less to do with medical risk than many of us have been led to expect.

You were also asked to determine which of your reasons for delaying a decision are purposive and which are contingent or emotional. Purposive reasons for delay are those that fall into the category of things to be accomplished before making the parenthood decision, such as completing an educational or training goal, accomplishing a career goal, or achieving financial independence or security. The common element among these goals is that they are measurable milestones in the life cycle; you know whether or not they have been achieved. In contrast, contingent goals are more difficult to assess. They tend to be "threshold" conditions that must be met before a decision can be faced; thus, although they may seem to be like some purposive goals, they are usually more vague, such as "when our relationship is more stable" or "when I feel more settled, or accomplished" or "not until he(she) wants a child as much as I do." There is no question that such contingent goals can be terribly important to those who have them, but determining whether and when they have been reached is subjective and often difficult.

The most subjective and elusive reasons for delay are those that have a strong emotional component. Although they may not be able to identify the source of their strong feelings, some people simply do not feel ready to face a decision about parenthood. Even if it is not possible to identify the components of such strong feelings, it is very valuable to recognize the legitimacy of their strength and their predictive power.

Assessing Your Reasons for Delay

It is necessary that you pull together your thoughts about delay before you can begin the decision-making process. First, rank your own reasons for delay, in order of their importance to you at present, according to the following categories:

1. Your most important reason for delay.
2. Other reasons for delay that are important to you.
3. Additional reasons for delay.

As an example, recall the case of Tom and Janet, presented in chapter 2. They are now in their middle thirties, and their ten-year delay since their marriage was primarily for purposive reasons: Tom was completing his professional specialty training, and both of them took the time necessary to become established in their respective careers. In accomplishing these goals, they have solidified their financial position, and they have also become, as they describe it, "comfortable" in their intimate relationship.

Contrast their situation with that of Diane and David, presented in the same chapter. Diane and David have also accomplished some career goals, but their working-class backgrounds and previous intimate relationships indicate that it was more of a struggle for them to reach their current situation. They are less sure of themselves and of each other. Their reasons for delaying a parenthood decision are characterized by much more uncertainty about their identities as individuals and about the future of their relationship together.

Now consider which of your reasons for delay are purposive. For the reasons that fit into this category, you should assess whether they have in fact been accomplished sufficiently for you to face making a decision about parenthood. If they have not yet been accomplished, you should try to estimate a reasonable timetable for each one and indicate when you think a decision point could be reached. When you have done this for the purposive reasons on your list, you will have begun to place your personal decision in a specific time frame.

The time frame for Janet and Tom's decision, for example, is pretty clear. Their purposes for delay have been accomplished, and further delay in facing a decision can only add to their concerns about increased risk of medical and genetic problems. If they eventually choose parenthood, added delay can also increase their financial burdens at the distant end of their timing for parenthood, as their children's college expenses would come near their time for retirement. For all of these reasons, the time for them to face a decision is now.

Deciding whether now is the time for facing a parenthood decision is much more complicated for Diane and David. They agree that they have made a great deal of progress, occupationally, personally, and in their relationship with each other, but there is more tentativeness and uncertainty in their tone when they describe their present situation and their concerns about the future. In part, this uncertainty exists because their situation is more complicated, but there are also other reasons for their hesitation. Diane, particularly, finds it difficult to identify which of her reasons for delay is most important to her. She is also concerned about the changes that parenthood would be likely to cause in her own life and in her relationship with her partner. In their past experience, parenting was women's work, but this is no longer acceptable to Diane as a personal model for parenthood. Therefore, part of her delay is contingent; that is, she can consider parenthood only if its responsibilities and rewards could be shared more equally with Tom. Diane's uncertainty is genuine. She is not sure whether Tom can accept a parenting role that is so radically different from the ones he has experienced. Also, she is not sure whether she could maintain the changed model she would like to have in her own parenthood situation, since her own experience provides no role models. Furthermore, she has seen friends begin parenthood with the same ideals but be unable to maintain them in the face of day-to-day demands and emergencies.

Now you should specify which of your reasons for delay are contingent. If you are in doubt about whether a reason can be categorized as contingent, try to state it as a condition for delaying a decision about parenthood "until" or "only if" something occurs or is true of your situation. Your assessment of contingent reasons for delay will necessarily be more subjective than that for your purposive reasons; use your own best guess. Each contingent reason can be assessed according to two factors: (1) the degree of importance to you and (2) the possibility for change—that is, your judgment of whether there is likely to be any change in the situation in the future. By combining these factors, you can use them in the following ways to help you reach a decision point:

1. For contingent reasons that can be assessed now because they are unlikely to change: determine their degree of importance to you, and then treat them as if they were purposive reasons, as discussed earlier, and use them in reaching your decision.
2. For contingent reasons that cannot be assessed now because you think they might change:
   a. If they are important to you, your "delay" may be permanent unless you can specify what can be worked on or changed.
   b. If they are not so important to you, your decision should be based on your other reasons for delay.

The case of Eleanor and Don in chapter 2 is an example of a delay situation that is primarily contingent. Eleanor is unwilling to face a decision about parenthood unless she can be certain that it could be combined satisfactorily with her presently satisfying career and intimate relationship. She does not want to repeat the experiences of her own mother. Although this couple is presently leaning away from parenthood, they are unwilling to make a definite decision because of the negative personal and social images associated with such a personal choice. With regard to the timing of their decision, none of these concerns is likely to change for them in the future; therefore, delaying their decision further can only buy them some temporary relief from the social pressures that concern them.

You should also ask yourself whether the contingent reasons that you ranked as important to you at present are as likely to be as important to you in the future. Personal priorities have a way of changing as the years pass and as our life paths develop and shift. Also, the opinions of others often become less important as we grow more certain of our own opinions. Recall the example of Anne, the professional woman of 40, who, at 20 or 30, would not have dreamed of considering parenthood outside the context of a stable marriage. Such a relationship has not become part of her life, however, and she now lives in a social environment in which single parenthood has advocates and even some successful practitioners. For her, the once-powerful reason to delay "unless" there was the right marriage has become less important; it has been superseded by considerations about her age and the stability of her own motivation and resources.

We defined the third category of concerns that lead to delay in facing a decision about parenthood as being associated with strong feelings. For example, in the case of Frank, presented in chapter 2, he was afraid that he might be the carrier of a genetic cause of the severe handicap that afflicted his younger sister, whose arrival brought such strain into his family. Also, some women who are concerned that they might not be good mothers describe that concern as strongly tinged with fear and distress recalled from their childhood memories. As one ambivalent woman told me, "It would be better to have no family at all than to repeat the one I grew up in."

Some of these primarily emotional reasons for delay can be converted into purposive ones. For example, Frank and his wife Sally could both undergo genetic testing and counseling, and the information provided might reassure them greatly, even if it could not provide absolute certainty that a child of theirs would be born free of handicaps. However, this would also require that they be able to persuade the family members involved (possibly including parents, siblings, and their spouses and children) to share the problem and cooperate with the genetic inquiries. The residue of guilt and avoidance builds up over the years with problems like these, and it can be both difficult and painful to break through the crust that is formed.

If your primary reason for delay has a strong emotional component, you should ask yourself, first, whether there is any factural information that might address your concerns. If there is (as there was for Frank and Sally), you then have to decide whether you wish to undertake the psychological and other costs of obtaining and facing that information. If you decide to go ahead with obtaining and using the information, that indicates that your motivation to face a decision about parenthood is strong and that it is likely to be worth the costs of the process for you to proceed, although it may not be easy. If you cannot imagine any factual information that would address your concerns, or if you are pessimistic about the relative costs of obtaining and using such information, your delay in facing a decision may be permanent. The most appropriate step for you now is to reconsider the meaning and importance of parenthood to you.

As we discussed earlier, it is premature to make a decision about parenthood until you have thought through what being a parent means to you. Only after you have decided what it would mean for you to be a parent (or a nonparent) for the next two decades can you face deciding whether you want it as part of your life now and in the future. The issue is not how much work being a parent will involve; responsible parenthood, like any other role, will require effort on your part. The question is how you view that effort. We all know people who work very hard yet derive great satisfaction and happiness from their work; we also know people who do as much or less but consider their work travail and drudgery. There is one crucial difference about the work of parenthood, however—namely, that children are people, not products. They may begin as small, helpless people, but they need more than just caretaking. Attention, respect, honesty, and encouragement are also part of the time-consuming job of bringing out the best in other people, whatever their age.

A young person who turns out to be a complete and happy individual is a pleasure to know, and parents of such a person are especially rewarded when this occurs. As anyone who works in human services will tell you, however, there are no guarantees that any person will turn out well, even with the best efforts of those who care and try to help. That, too, is part of parenthood and part of the chance you take; your very best efforts may not result in what you had hoped for and dreamed of as a parent. That is why optimism and a healthy amount of faith and self-confidence help so much in parenting; if you take all the rough stretches personally or, worse yet, don't allow for any difficult stretches as part of the job, then you may find parenthood a serious disappointment.

A professional woman with unusual psychological insight spoke on this theme to my class in decision making. She described her concern that a "late" child of hers might be born with major defects and her fears that late parenthood was not the "right" decision. Her period of tense uncertainty and ambivalence was relieved greatly, however, after she had a powerful dream that enabled her to accept whatever she would get as a parent, even if it was less than perfect. Thus, she did not change her perspective about what parenthood would mean to her on the basis of more information; rather, the change was in her attitude about whether she could handle the full range of possible outcomes that might come with parenthood.

Two other kinds of intangible changes in the timing and pattern of decision making happen surprisingly often. First, for no specific reasons that they can later identify, some people who have been comfortable with delaying a decision about parenthood more or less indefinitely notice rather suddenly that they are much more aware of the children they see around them. As one man told me, "Suddenly I was stopping to watch and visit with little kids and their parents—I never did that before." His wife added, "He would just get right down in the market checkout line and visit with toddlers he had never noticed before, so I wasn't too surprised when he began talking about what having one of our own might be like." For this couple, the issue changed from "if" to "when and how," primarily because the man's feelings about parenthood changed, relatively independently of other circumstances in their lives.

The second type of situation occurs when people who have been pretty careful about contraception for many years either become less careful or experience one of the "failures" in the odds associated with each method. It is frequently impossible to say which has occurred, but suddenly there is a pregnancy, and a decision must be made whether to continue with it or not. Many adults of all ages choose to terminate such "surprises," but some of the most enthusiastic and committed later-life parents are those who joined the ranks of parents in this relatively inadvertent manner. The details of how such unlikely conceptions occur are not as important as the subsequent reaction to them. Such parents have reported to me that although they were surprised at the news, they were even more surprised at their reaction to it, compared to what they had expected. As one woman said:

> This happened before, when I was 24. I was really upset, but I felt I had to go ahead and get an abortion. Although I knew then that it was the best thing for me to do, it was really difficult in those days and it took me a long time to get over it. Now, although some of my friends led me to think that I should be somewhat embarrassed at my age, secretly I am really delighted. It's like fate has given me another chance, and I'm brave or crazy enough to want to take it, even at this stage. I would never have planned this, and certainly not at 42, but now that it has happened, it really is wonderful!

When I asked her how she would have described herself with regard to possible parenthood before the event, she said that she would have been pretty firmly in the permanently childless category. Her life at 42 was busy and satisfying, and most of her friends who were parents had children who were grown and nearly on their own. She had been married for many years to a man whose feelings about parenthood she described as "vague at best, but now that he is going to be a father, he's more excited and terrified than I am.

He's reading, to become an instant expert, talking about getting a bigger house, or one in the country, even wondering if it is too early to start buying toys."

These examples are not rare occurrences. They may be difficult to tally according to established statistical methods, but they are part of the experience of too many of us to be ignored. What they point out is a useful counterbalance to any effort to be too systematic about this major decision. Although it is important to assess the pros and cons of your own decision as carefully and thoroughly as you can, it is also important to continue to recognize that a decision about parenthood is also a decision of the heart. Your summary assessment of your reasons for delaying a decision could lead to one of several approaches at this point. For most people, they will indicate the merit of trying to reach a decision now, even though everything may not be clear and ambivalence remains. For some, however, there will be sufficient remaining purposive reasons to defer reaching a decision; in this case, the reasons and the timetable for the deferral should be as specific as you can make them. If you are among those who still do not feel ready to face a decision—and you don't know when you will feel ready—the discussion that follows should help you clarify why you still feel unready.

Summarizing the Relevant Decision-Making Considerations

We will proceed now to integrate the information you have accumulated on the medical, social, and personal aspects of the parenthood decision. Exercise 6 provides a format within which you may summarize your information and your reactions to it (or use any other format that will help you concentrate on these essential dimensions of choice):

1. First, indicate the aspects of your own physical, occupational, social, and personal situation that are important in your decision about parenthood.
2. For each of these factors, determine whether they indicate that a choice of parenthood or nonparenthood would be better for you now or in the future.
3. If you and a partner are facing this decision together, the next level of consideration is the extent of your agreement in your summary so far. Where and how strongly do you agree or disagree?
4. What is your emotional reaction to this summary? Objectively, the various considerations may add up to indicate a yes or a no on parenthood at this stage; how does this feel?

Exercise 6
Decision-Making Summary

Relevant Considerations	Yes or No		Extent of Partner Agreement	Reactions, Feelings
	Now?	*Future?*		
Medical/genetic:				
Occupational:				
Social:				
Personal:				

Use as much detail and weighting of items as you feel will be useful to you in reaching a decision. When you have completed the summary, think a while about anything else that might be relevant, and make additions if necessary.

Now, turn your paperwork over, look squarely at your partner or into a mirror and make that decision—yes, no, or still undecided. If there is little doubt or disagreement, you may wish to proceed to the appropriate section of this chapter for your decision. If things are less certain or more controversial at this point, read on. If timing is the issue (you are fairly sure how you have decided but not when or for how long), you should read the "undecided" section and either the "yes" or the "no" section, depending on your tentative decision. If the issue is disagreement between you and your partner, however, more discussion and further negotiation will probably be necessary. If one partner is still undecided and the other has made a yes or no choice, a mutual review of your assessments of your situations and timing may be useful. Some partners who disagree have found it helpful to use outside resources—for example, organizations such as Resolve (see the resource section at the end of this book)—to discuss the issues with others who are facing similar dilemmas. You may also find professional counseling to be helpful. Such counseling is strongly advised if you and your partner have reached opposite decisions—one a definite yes and the other a just-as-definite no. In this situation, you will need to address the importance and the future of your relationship, taking into account the relative importance of the parenthood decision to that future.

What to Do If You Are Still Undecided

You have assessed your current situation but find that when you add up all the considerations involved, you are still unable to make a firm positive or negative decision about parenthood. On the assumption that no one wants to remain undecided forever, this section presents some options that may help you in this state of uncertainty:

1. First, try to be as clear and specific as possible about the reasons you remain undecided about parenthood.
2. Second, try to establish a timetable for your uncertainty—determining when to review your options for choice again.
3. Third, to facilitate your adjustment to uncertainty, try to find support for your feelings and obtain additional information or resources if possible.

Reasons for Remaining Undecided

No one wants to spend an indefinite period of time sitting on the fence. While you're uncertain, however, it does help to have clear reasons why you continue to be so for the present. By now, you have had plenty of opportunities to determine the combination of circumstances that has put you into the undecided group. However, these circumstances may not be the same as the ones that now cause you to remain there or the ones that will determine how long you are likely to stay there. Some common themes have been raised by people like you; although only one of these themes may be mentioned, they overlap to some extent.

The reason for uncertainty that is most commonly mentioned by younger people who are deferring a decision is that they are not yet ready. They give various reasons for this unreadiness, but the most common reason is that they are still in the process of achieving some specific goals. Among people in their thirties and forties, however, the goals mentioned often reflect a career transition or some other major change in their lives. They are starting over in some major way, and feel that they need time to complete or adjust to the transition. This is a very reasonable cause for deferral of choice. If unreadiness is your primary reason, but you want to proceed toward making a choice while there is still time, you should establish a date not too far in the future (perhaps six months or a year from now) when you will reevaluate your progress.

This step is particularly important for couples in which one partner feels sure of his or her choice but the other is undecided for this reason. A realistic and sincere agreement to review the situation at an agreed-upon time often reduces tension and friction, permitting a less emotional discussion of other issues involved in the decision.

The "unreadiness" reason often overlaps with another reason—namely, that the current environmental situation is not right for making a decision. It may be that the economy is uncertain (and, therefore, your job is uncertain) or that relocation may be necessary. With the increasing number of second marriages, the environmental uncertainty may be on a more personal level, such as, "We don't know if my (his/her) kids will be staying with us or not." Most of the "environmental" reasons given for uncertainty may be seen as tentatively negative decisions about parenthood. They are negative in the immediate sense, of course, because the implication is that you cannot begin consideration of parenthood under such uncertain circumstances. Furthermore, to the extent that such circumstances have no clear duration (the economy is always uncertain), these reasons can remain negative choices indefinitely.

Thus, if you do not want to just drift into a decision for nonparenthood, it is necessary that you put some limits on your consideration of environmental circumstances. What will you do if the economy is still uncertain a year from now? You can make a specific plan or seek a more secure environmental situation in the interim. For example, you can make alternative plans for decisions that allow for either the presence or the absence of children from previous marriages, or you can make an active decision to arrange or rearrange your living arrangements so that a decision about parenthood is possible.

The Timing of Uncertainty

Continuing in a state of uncertainty means that you are spending both time and energy avoiding coming to grips with a decision. Uncertainty involves a great deal of emotional tension, and the waiting and worrying can be worse than working through to a decision. Both uncertainty and decision making involve effort on your part, but delay gives you nothing to show for the effort, and the passage of time is not reassuring if you are already concerned that the biological clock is ticking away. Few of us ever have all the information we need to be absolutely sure about making the right decision. For some of us, claiming a lack of information represents another avoidance strategy. Consider, for example, the person who cannot decide until the "right" partner comes along, yet has no clear idea of what "right" means to him or her.

Living with major uncertainties makes it much more difficult to get on with the rest of your life as well, planning for and carrying out other life plans that are important to you. Furthermore, as anyone who has been delayed in a dentist's waiting room knows, uncertainty does not become more comfortable as time passes. In sum, the message on timing is to establish a time frame—if at all possible in the near future—when you will again review your decision situation. Things may well look different to you in a year; even if they don't, your feelings about them or about parenthood may change with the passage of time.

Living with the Present Uncertainty

For the present, your uncertainty about the parenthood decision needs to be kept at a manageable level. Use whatever coping strategies work for you to reduce the tension and distraction that inevitably arise at times. Do not spend any more time than necessary in situations that push you toward a decision before you feel that you are ready. You can find support for your feelings by talking with others who are uncertain. If your uncertainty is part of a more general problem with making decisions about things in your life and acting on them, professional therapists and groups are available to help you. Similarly, if disagreement with your partner is a major component of your uncertainty and delay, you (and your relationship) may be helped through professional counseling.

In any case, continue to remind yourself, and others if necessary, that you are doing the best thing for the present by admitting your uncertainty, rather than pushing yourself or being pushed into a decision or action for which you feel unprepared. The worst that can happen, as noted earlier, is that your temporary nonparenthood will become more permanent. The alternative—parenthood—is a large and permanent life change, so if something inside you still says to wait, it is a good idea to do so.

What to Do If You Have Decided to Remain Childless

You have assessed your current and future situations as thoroughly and honestly as you know how, and you have concluded that, for you, the best choice is to remain permanently childless. What can you do, now and in the future, to affirm and support your decision?

1. First, you can specify all the affirmative reasons for your decision.
2. Second, you can explore any remaining concerns you have about your decision, especially those that have to do with the nurturing side of your nature and the pronatalist social pressures you may be facing; help is available.

3. Third, you should begin to use this decision to help you plan your future as a childfree person.

Affirmation of Your Choice to Be Childless

Affirmation of your choice is particularly important for you because of the relatively unique status you have chosen. The problem is not that your life so far has involved doing what everyone else is doing; if that were true, you would not be facing such a decision about parenthood now. Rather, developing a positive approach to any decision is a much more effective way of reinforcing your success in implementing that decision than merely marshalling reasons why you did not choose another alternative. You would not describe your choice of a mate or a career by saying that the other choices were worse and giving specific reasons. Yet the pronatalist cultural perspective in which we live leads us to describe a choice to be childless in such terms—for example, that we know or fear that we would not be good parent material. You may, indeed, fear that you would not be an ideal parent, but fear or guilt are not going to give you the best start in feeling positive about the decision you have reached and going ahead with the rest of your life.

Instead, you should emphasize all the positive aspects of your present childless situation. Be specific, also, about what you can and will work toward becoming in your future as a childfree person. This may seem to be a relatively novel approach, partly because you have not seen it applied very often. Twenty years ago, however, editor and writer Gael Greene took the startlingly affirmative stance in a major magazine that she had chosen to remain childfree to "champion the wondrously satisfying love of a woman and her husband, two adults enjoying the knowledge and mystery of each other, tasting dependence, accepting responsibility, yet individual and free."[1] Although you may not read much about them, in the 1980s there are many couples who are equals in their dependence on and independence of each other. Both partners may pursue careers, not just because of the financial advantages but also because each of them values the success and the sense of growth and personal accomplishment from his or her work. If your life is like this, and if parenthood is not part of your plans, be assured that there are others like you and that there is more social support for your choices now than in the past.

Another positive theme among the childfree is personal freedom.[2] Do you enjoy the ability to be flexible, to change, to take risks, to move quickly when the opportunity presents itself, or to follow a creative impulse wherever it may lead you? People like you are among our most creative and original innovators, artists, and explorers of new areas. Also, the availability of such people can be invaluable when disaster strikes or when emergencies arise.

Some of the most realistic people I have met in our age cohort have taken another positive approach to voluntary childlessness. They have chosen lives that are rewarding to them, even if their choices of jobs or other aspects of their life plan mean that they will never be affluent or even well off. For such people, parenthood would be a near-impossible burden, both financially and emotionally, because they would have to choose between their current lives and the additional demands that come with parenthood. They know that social circumstances at present do not make it easy for parents of young children, financially or in terms of available services, and that finding affordable child care would be very difficult. Furthermore, they could not afford to pay their basic bills if either partner stopped working to care for children. Such people are no longer committed to parenthood at any cost, even if they might like to be. In other times, when mixing parenthood with the life they have chosen would be more feasible, they probably would become parents. Indeed, in the last generation, many of them did, because in those days people were not expected to worry about the costs of parenthood when they began their families, even if they had good cause to do so. Now, however, forgoing parenthood is a positive and voluntary choice that people make to be able to maintain the lifestyle they value.

Deciding to remain childless is neither straightforward or easy for many people. Even if you are reasonably certain that nonparenthood is the best choice for you, the reactions and expectations of other people may lead even the most reasonable of you to have troubling second thoughts. If you have felt such pressures, several approaches to coping with them might be helpful.

The first approach is to be aware that most outsiders' questions and suggestions, though well motivated, reflect some lack of knowledge about your particular situation. You are a better judge of your life choices, precisely because you have reviewed your choice options more thoroughly. The best (some would say the only) reason to choose parenthood is because you have decided that you are prepared to go ahead with it; the reasons others might give you can range from weak to downright poor justifications for choosing parenthood. You may have encountered some of the reasons satirized in some television advertisements:

(older couple)	You've been married for quite a while now. When are we going to see grandchildren?
(woman)	Why knock myself out working when I can have a baby and stay home?
(man)	Hey, buddy, what are you and the little woman waiting for? No problem in bed, eh?
(couple)	We want a boy, to keep the family name going.
(woman)	Have a baby? What else is a woman for?
(man)	You want a baby? OK, we'll have a baby—maybe that'll patch things up.[3]

People who become parents for other people's reasons—or to become something they would like to be but are not—may have ample time for regret, but they will have little opportunity for reconsideration of their parenthood. If you get such pressure from others, you can respond in several ways. The most difficult approach is to try to educate them in return, pointing out the advantages of nonparenthood. It is often easier, however, not to confront such deeply held prejudices in others but simply to state that your choice is made and that you won't try to change their minds if they won't try to change yours. Alternatively, some couples allow others to conclude that their childlessness is involuntary rather than by personal choice; this alternative tends to stifle further discussion, because people are reluctant to recognize or discuss handicaps of any kind. In any case, there is some comfort in knowing that this kind of social pressure tends to diminish with the passage of time.

Concerns about the Future

Many people who have few doubts about their choice of a childless life now and in the immediate future still wonder how they will feel about not having children (and hence possible grandchildren) when they are older. This concern is often reinforced from two directions. One such reinforcement is the pervasive media image of beloved, well-groomed, healthy grandparents being visited, feted, phoned, and sent flowers by their equally attractive descendants. Such media presentations, especially during major holiday seasons, may gladden the hearts of the telephone, greeting card, and florist industries, but they may have nothing to do with your own family experiences. Even in families that are close and achieve enduring, warm relationships across generations, there is room for childless aunts and uncles. Furthermore, for many older people, relationships with their children and grandchildren are less than ideal; the most unfortunate of all are those who do not get the attention they expect from their offspring. One 65-year-old acquaintance, whose childfree life has been full of humor and accomplishment, told me that she feels sorry for such friends of hers on holidays but that she has no time to feel sorry for herself; her holidays are busy visiting friends or taking advantage of travel bargains that cannot be used by those she describes as having to "stay home and cook."

Moving Ahead to Action on Your Decision

One of the first actions you should consider is an assessment of the methods of contraception you have been using to determine whether they are the best methods for you to continue using in the future. Each of the commonly used methods for temporary contraception has both direct risk (pregnancy) and indirect risk associated with it. There is voluminous research literature, for example, on the increased risk of cardiovascular disease associated with prolonged use of oral contraceptives. Also, intrauterine devices increase the risk of several types of disorders of the reproductive system and are also associated with increased risk of pelvic inflammatory disease. There are only two safe methods for permanent contraception: abstinence and surgical interference with or removal of at least some portion of the reproductive system in either partner. The alternatives that physicians most often recommend for permanent contraception are vasectomy for men or tubal ligation for women. Each of these involves a relatively minor surgical procedure that can now be done in a physician's office or on an outpatient basis. Vasectomy interrupts the vas deferens, which carries sperm from the testes to the rest of the reproductive tract. Tubal ligation clamps or severs a portion of each fallopian tube, preventing mature egg cells from moving from the ovaries to the womb. Many couples consider vasectomy preferable for several reasons. First, the procedure is less complicated, which also means that there is less discomfort afterwards. It also means that if there is a later decision change, the odds of success for a procedure to reverse the vasectomy by reconnecting the vas deferens (called a vasovasectomy) are greater.

Another form of "insurance" against reconsideration is available for men who choose to have a vasectomy. Before having the procedure done, they can have sperm samples frozen and stored at very low temperatures indefinitely. The popular press has made much of the sperm bank option as part of efforts by a few people to produce superior offspring, but sperm banks are used primarily by men who are facing procedures that may permanently alter their chances for fertility (such as treatment for cancer) or by those who donate sperm so that women whose partners are infertile can conceive through artificial insemination.

Reversal of any sterilization procedure for either men or women is much more difficult and expensive than the original procedure, and the odds for a successful outcome are less than 50 percent. The chances of a successful reversal for women are much less than those for men. Also, although the majority of vas deferens reconnections do permit passage of sperm, problems associated with the duration of time since the vasectomy can still reduce the chances for successful conception. Counseling prior to sterilization is advised by most practitioners and medical insurers (and is required by many) as an effort to provide an opportunity for those who are considering such a procedure to face fully the seriousness and permanence of going ahead with it.

Remaining childless does not mean giving up your need or opportunities to be a nurturing person. Most people who are sure that parenthood is not for them are still able to be nurturing in other ways. If one of your concerns for the future is to satisfy your needs as a nurturing person, there are many opportunities to make good use of the nurturing resources you have to give. The most readily available opportunity is often within your own extended family group. Many of us were lucky enough to have a favorite aunt or uncle who could be a trusted adult friend and confidant, interested in us but not a parent, with all the rules and limits of that role. I had such an aunt and uncle when I was growing up, and the time I spent with them was very special for me, even when we didn't do anything special. A single career woman told one of my classes how gratified she was by her role as "older sister" and aunt to her adolescent nephews and nieces who were negotiating the difficult transition away from home and parents. By staying with her, they were able to consider and discuss alternatives and choices to be made without the pressures to do the "right thing" that they received at home.

This special role of adult who is nurturing, supportive, and interested, but not a parent, is one of the major losses resulting from the demise of the extended family system in our society. Its unique value is recognized, however, by an organization that matches children, especially those from single-parent homes, with adult "Big Brothers" or "Big Sisters" who volunteer their services. As a Big Brother or Big Sister, you agree to spend some of your leisure time with your Little Sister or Little Brother on a fairly regular basis, doing things that both of you enjoy. You don't have to be rich or have child care experience to be special to a child who has only one hard-working parent and, frequently, no other family members who think that he or she is special. Most cities have Big Brother/Big Sister organizations, and they would be delighted to hear from you.

There are many other ways to volunteer your caring abilities and interests. All of the youth organizations, such as Boy Scouts, Campfire Girls, and community- and church-sponsored groups, need adults with and without special skills to share their time with the children in their programs. If you are interested in sports, for example, coaches for baseball, swimming, soccer, football, and other team sports for young people don't have to be parents.

If you have the emotional strength, you might join some of the most important and appreciated volunteer caregivers I have known—people who donate their all-too-scarce "laps" to hold and rock children who are in institutions because of prolonged illness or severe mental or physical handicaps. If you call any of these institutions or a local volunteer-coordinating service, you will find that there is more need than you can imagine; any time or effort you can give would be greatly appreciated. Besides putting your nurturing ability to good use, such activities will help you put your own problems in the proper perspective.

Finally, now that you have climbed out of the sticky web of ambivalence and indecision, consider the much wider horizons you have for deciding what to do with the rest of your life. Now that no cultural requirement for parenthood binds you, the opportunities to develop and explore and change may be so open that they are almost frightening. You have chosen the easiest path to accomplishment; it might be faster and easier to have a baby than to write that book, paint that picture, or accomplish your own difficult, time-consuming goal. To work toward accomplishing all that your abilities allow is not just the best use of your time and energies, however; it is also the best antidote to the stereotypes of selfishness and immaturity that are still applied to those who remain childless. There would be more satisfied and fulfilled people in our society if we not only encouraged those who want to be parents to do it well but also encouraged those who do not want to be parents to be whatever they want to be with equal enthusiasm. The availability of more alternatives can mean more selective, happier parenthood and nonparenthood, to the benefit of us all.

What to Do If You Have Chosen Parenthood

You have thoroughly and realistically reviewed your present situation and considered what you would like your future to be, and you have concluded that you want parenthood to be part of that future. First—congratulations; this is not an easy decision to have reached in these times. As you may have surmised, much of this book has deliberately portrayed the potential costs as well as the rewards of parenthood, so that you could face this major decision realistically. Right now, you probably feel both excited and apprehensive. Not only is this combination of powerful feelings to be expected now, but you may as well get used to it, since such feelings are typical much of the time throughout pregnancy and even well into parenthood. It is interesting, though, that one thing you cannot anticipate, no matter how well prepared for parenthood you try to be, is the intensity and range of feelings and emotions that come with parenthood. One mother described it thus:

> I'd been deeply in love before, but there was never a love like this one! I was on clouds, in the depths, tearful with joy at the tiniest things. Sometimes we were almost drowned in waves of feeling.

And a father who is deeply committed to pacifism said to me the day after his child was born: "Now I know why animals can kill to defend their young."

A great deal of help and support is available to you in beginning to plan for parenthood, and the time to begin finding out about it and making use of it is now, even if you do not plan to embark on parenthood right away. This section presents an outline for a plan of action, including information on available resources. The plan includes the following components:

1. First, consider the parenthood timing you would prefer, taking into account the likelihood of more delay than you have planned. Child spacing is part of this decision if you plan to have more than one child.

2. As soon as possible, review your physiological state of preparation for parenthood. This should include an examination of your own health habits and behavior and an up-to-date medical review of your general and reproductive status.
3. Consider whether your commitment to parenthood includes only natural or biological parenthood, or whether you will plan for alternatives such as adoption if necessary.
4. Begin to plan and obtain information about the best possible fit between parenthood and the rest of your activities. Arrangements for job leave or change, child care, and financial and other resources will require as much advance planning as you can give them.

Many books have been written on each aspect of the action plan outlined here. All that I intend here is to raise issues that you will want to consider from your relatively unique position as mature potential parents. I will often direct you to the resources section at the end of the book, where suggestions for further reading and lists of organizations that can help are provided according to subject areas.

Timing Considerations

You may have already considered some parenthood timing issues as part of your decision-making process. For example, if there are slow cycles in your work schedule or anticipated natural breaks in your career timing, the earliest part of your parenthood would be easier at such quieter times, if it is possible for you to arrange it. Within the timing plan that seems to fit your situation best, however, you may wish to consider several additional points.

First, are you considering having more than one child? If you are, a delay in timing for the first child will affect your planning throughout your parenthood cycle. Furthermore, you should consider the age you are likely to be when you have your last child as well as when you have your first. There are also child-spacing options to consider. You might prefer to delay having your first child somewhat but allow only about two years before the second; or you might find it more sensible to have the first child promptly but delay the second for a longer period. If you are nearer 40 than 30, these relatively leisurely considerations may seem to be luxuries you cannot afford.

None of the foregoing discussion should be considered an encouragement or even an implication that mature parents should have more than one child. Although there is a great deal of folklore about the misery of the only child, there is virtually no evidence to support it. To the contrary, there are research findings that only children are happier and grow and develop better than children who have siblings. Furthermore, many parents report that although some adjustment was necessary with the arrival of their first child, their real problems began when they had more than one.

However many children you may wish to have, you should be aware that several studies have found that it takes longer, on the average, for older people to conceive once they start trying.[4] It is not unusual for it to take six months to a year for an older woman to become pregnant—even longer for women who have been taking oral contraceptives. Thus, although you might be the exception who succeeds promptly in beginning your parenthood, chances are that even if you decide to go ahead promptly, the actual event will be somewhat delayed.

Most specialists in infertility advise that you try for at least a year before you seek their services. For people these specialists are able to help, there may be an additional delay of months or years until the problem is identified and treatment has time to take effect. Finally, for those who ultimately decide that biological parenthood is not going to be their lot in life, adoption delays can take additional months or years. (See the later discussion of alternatives to biological parenthood and the resources section at the end of the book.) Considering all these potential delays, parenthood may occur for you much later than you had planned. Therefore, unless there are important reasons to the contrary, if you're really ready for parenthood, don't wait too long to get started.

Physical Preparation for Parenthood

You are part of a generation that is also unique in a way other than the ones we have already discussed. Positive and active efforts on the part of many of you to achieve and maintain good physical health have contributed to a more dramatic improvement in the health of our population than any of the much publicized advances in medical care over the last two decades. During my career in public health, I have helped to conduct and analyze research studies demonstrating the positve effects of the decline in smoking, improved nutritional habits, and greater attention to physical fitness. If you are already taking an active personal role in your own optimal health status, I encourage you to continue this activity into and throughout your parenthood. Your good health habits will help make your transition to parenthood easier and more successful. Chapter 3 presented evidence of the effects of parental health status on the course of pregnancy and delivery. These health effects actually begin even earlier, in the sense that people who are severely overweight or underweight, or who smoke or drink heavily, have less success in even becoming pregnant, partly because these factors affect their production of the hormones that control fertility.

Your planning for parenthood should include a thorough assessment of your physical condition before you begin. Schedule a complete physical examination for yourself (and your partner), more than just a check of your various organ systems and routine laboratory tests of blood and urine. Such an examination could turn up early symptoms of chronic diseases that can be controlled through changes in your health habits rather than through drug interventions that might be contraindicated in pregnancy. This means that you should entrust your health to a professional who cares about lifestyle and health habits and can advise you on maintaining habits that will maximize your good health status throughout parenthood. Remember, also, that your children will learn health habits from you.

If you are concerned about the difficulty of changing old habits that you know are not good for your health, it may help you to know that many people have been helped by parenthood in their resolve to change for the better. The responsibility for another life is a very powerful influence for change. Parents who smoke, for example, must now face the knowledge that their children's health is also negatively affected by their smoking.

Of course, part of your physical assessment should be a check of your reproductive system, including, in addition to a physical examination, a review of your reproductive history and your use of contraception. You should also expect to be asked about any family history of problems with or diseases of the reproductive system. You should make it clear at the outset that you are planning parenthood, so that potential problems associated with conception and pregnancy can be part of the examination. Again, for planning purposes it is a good idea to ask your physician to recommend specialists in both infertility and high-risk pregnancy, even though the chances are that you will not need the services of either.

Much has been written recently about the spectre of infertility. For example, a recent editorial in a prestigious medical journal argued that women should not be swayed by career considerations to defer pregnancy until they are older, simply because the chances of infertility increase with age.[5] To determine whether you are at greater risk of infertility problems, there are several indicators you should consider before you attempt pregnancy. For women, the most common characteristics that could contribute to a greater likelihood of infertility include the following:

1. A history of pelvic inflammatory disease (PID), especially if it required hospital treatment. There are many causes of PID, but once there is infection, the resulting adhesions or scar tissue can interfere with the normal function of the reproductive system.
2. A history of endometriosis. Here, the problem is caused by endometrial tissue that has migrated from the uterus and attaches itself elsewhere in the pelvic area. The results can be similar to those of PID—adhesions, scarring, or cysts, which can cause blockage around the ovaries and fallopian tubes. Such problems may be treated with hormones or, in severe cases, by surgery.
3. Any major gynocological surgery, such as surgery for removal of ovarian cysts or benign fibroid growths in the uterus.
4. Conization of the cervix because of cervical dysplasia or as a follow-up

of a borderline Pap test. This can lead to cervical stenosis, or blockage of the cervical canal. Stenosis might also be congenital or might result from infection or injury. In any case, it may impair the ability of sperm to travel through the cervical canal.

5. A previous history of infertility with another sexual partner, including any prolonged period when you were sexually active without using contraception and did not become pregnant.

For men, the most common indicators of possible fertility problems include the following:

1. Variocele, or varicose veins in the scrotal sac, which affects the formation of sperm cells.
2. Exposure to toxic environmental agents, including not only occupational exposures but chemotherapy and even any drugs your mother might have taken when she was pregnant with you. (These exposures are the most difficult to diagnose and the least likely to be correctible.)
3. Previous urogenital area surgery, especially for undescended testicle, or bladder neck surgery.
4. A history of mumps during adolescence or later.
5. A previous history of infertility with another sexual partner, including any prolonged period when you were sexually active without using contraception and did not cause pregnancy.

Some dramatic new techniques are being used to diagnose and correct many of these problems. Analyses of the complex cycles of hormonal influences on ovulation, sperm production, and conception can now identify and help treat problems that could not even be diagnosed accurately until recently. Furthermore, microsurgery and laser surgical techniques are now being used to clear adhesions and scarring in such complicated areas as the vas deferens and the fallopian tubes. Also, since the first successful "test tube" birth in 1978 in England, hundreds of babies have been born who were conceived outside their mother's bodies and then implanted surgically to complete gestation.[6] Not all cases of infertility can be helped, however, and of the people who are helped, not all succeed in becoming biological parents. Diagnosis of and treatment for infertility can be prolonged, very expensive, frustrating, and ultimately disappointing. Therefore, it would be wise to consider, also, your position on the alternatives to biological parenthood.

Alternatives to Biological Parenthood

Most people over 30 who consider adopting children do so as an unexpected alternative to their plans for a natural family. Only after a more or less prolonged, frustrating period of trying to conceive do they face a decision about adoption. Unfortunately, many people discover at that point that there are many unforeseen obstacles in the path to adoption. The following discussion is designed to help you anticipate some of these obstacles, so that you can include them in your consideration of adoptive parenthood and anticipate strategies for overcoming them if you decide that adoption will be part of your plans for parenthood.

First, because of the escalating demand for and the drastically diminished supply of adoptable babies, adoption agencies are able to set very restrictive standards for adoptive parents, one of which is age. The agencies apparently believe that infants belong with younger parents, because the statistical norm for parenthood is still under age 30. One could reasonably argue that people over 30 are better prepared to become parents in terms of maturity and economic and marital stability, but the fact is that many agencies will not even process applications from people over 35. If you really want to adopt an infant or a young child, and you are much past 30, you should be prepared for an uphill fight.

If you are willing to adopt an older child, or two or more children from the same family, or a child who is handicapped or of a mixed racial background, your chances for success are much better, because it is more difficult to find homes for such children, even though the costs of medical or special care for handicapped children are covered in most states. Single parents, or those who are themselves handicapped, will find that becoming adoptive parents is even more difficult, regardless of their willingness to adopt even difficult-to-place children.

In any case, all adoption agencies will screen your ability and motivation to be a parent in the following ways (agencies that are affiliated with religious or ethnic groups may also set additional standards):

1. They will explore why you want to adopt. Your response should reflect the best interests of the child, not other interests, such as your personal needs or those of your marriage. They will also explore how you feel about being unable to be a biological parent, so that they can be sure that you do not see yourself and an adopted child as failures or second-best choices.
2. They will explore your willingness to adopt a child other than an infant without handicaps. You should make a sincere personal assessment of this decision before you are asked. There are no "right" answers; you just have to assess what you think you can handle.
3. They will explore your other qualifications for providing a good, stable parental environment, including financial, housing, physical, and psychological assessments of your capacity for parenthood.

In a sense, it is unfortunate that all potential parents do not have to pass some sort of screening for their readiness for parenthood. Rates of child neglect and abuse undoubtedly would be reduced significantly even if only the most obviously unsuited were identified. However, adoption agencies use statistically based norms, which means that people who have had periods of occupational or marital instability, even if they are now stable, and those who are unmarried or recently married may be rejected as candidates for parenthood at any age, but especially if they are over 30.

Alternative adoption methods do exist. One is independent adoption, which is often arranged through physicians, lawyers, or other family members. Such adoptions are illegal in some areas, for good reasons. Since neither the biological nor the adoptive parents are screened, the chances of later complications are greatly increased; there are many horror stories of adults who changed their minds, bringing litigation, expense, and heartbreak to child and parents. People with experience in trying to salvage and resolve these no-win situations advise very strongly against independent adoption. If you are tempted by such an opportunity, remember that if anything goes wrong, you will have few legal rights and a great deal to lose, often including a child that you have come to love.

Another alternative is adopting a child from another country. Many countries in Asia and Latin America have active adoption liaison arrangements with this country, often through the auspices of religious and charitable organizations that have missions and orphanages in those countries. For such adoptions, you will have to go through the legalities for both immigration and adoption; arrangements vary from country to country and from agency to agency. Some couples obtain children in this way with less expense and delay than they had expected after their experiences with local agencies, but others report at least as much delay, red tape, and expense as for other alternatives. Resource agencies for international adoptions can help you with information and advice, and some provide an opportunity to meet with parents who have used their services (see the resources section).

There is no question that an adopted child can bring as much love and joy into a family as a biological child, and you would have the added satisfaction of sharing the special gift of yourself. If adoption seems to require too much trouble and expense, however, you should examine your own motives again. Remember, too, that the efforts of adoption professionals are directed toward the same goals you have—ensuring the best possible parental environment for every child.

Fitting Parenthood into the Rest of Your Life

Since many books are available on this subject, this section will only mention some essential points that are especially relevant for more mature potential parents, including consideration of the stage you have reached in your own life cycle, taking charge of the universal and primary concern for quality child care, financial considerations, and adaptation to transitions.

First, you are part of a group that is farther along in the life cycle than the typical people to whom most of the "Hooray—you're pregnant!" books are addressed. The writers of these books may know a great deal about parenthood in general, but they don't know much about you—your experience, needs, priorities, and organizing abilities. Therefore, you should read what they have to say through the filter of your own self-knowledge and experience. Before you become a parent, you have to decide what you need from parenthood and from the rest of your life. It will be easier to make room in your life for parenthood if you determine ahead of time where there is some give in your current activities.

You must plan for both the large-scale and the small-scale demands of parenthood. By large-scale, I mean issues regarding who takes how much time off from work for parenthood and whether you will really be able to set aside the 20 to 25 percent of your income that experts anticipate as the cost of a first child from before pregnancy through the child's college years. By small-scale, I mean the day-to-day details and scheduling that should be planned for, at least in principle, before a child arrives, even though they may need to be much more flexible than you imagine.

The first large-scale question is how you will deal with the most demanding initial period of parenthood. You have three resources: yourself, other family members, and paid caretakers. (If you are a single parent, you may have fewer family options, and you may have to be more resourceful about arranging for alternative caretakers.) Basically, you will have to develop a plan that lies somewhere between what you think you should do or would like to do and what you think is realistically possible, taking into account other realities, such as limits of job leave and finances. You can be more rational about this now than after you are a parent, when sleep deprivation alone can diminish your ability to think clearly.

If you and your partner would prefer to share in this early period of parenthood, can both of your work schedules be flexible enough to permit such sharing? The time to explore such options is as far in advance of the event as possible. Unfortunately, most employers have little experience (or enthusiasm) for helping you work out your plans. Before you can approach them, however, you must discuss and agree on your own commitments and responsibilities.

Those of you who plan to join the ranks of fathers must allow for transitions and adjustments that may be among the most significant in your life. Our culture prepares women from childhood for the changes that come with parenthood, but men are generally left out of such preparation. This knowledge of the demands of parenthood and acceptance of an active part in it has traditionally been part of the work and world of women, so that even men who are willingly and actively good at parenting have had few ways of sharing their knowledge and enthusiasm with others.

Fortunately for us all, and especially for the next generation, this situation is gradually changing. If your personal definition of fatherhood includes more than going out and bringing home the proverbial bacon, but you don't know how to go about being a more active and involved parent, there are many helpful resources, including books for fathers and expectant fathers, such as *The Fathers Almanac,*[7] that contain advice, social support, and humor to help you along. There are also classes that you can take before you become a parent, so that you will know what to expect and how you can take an active parenthood role by the time events really get under way. These classes also function as support groups, helping you share a new and major part of your life. There are also special programs for fathers, such as those sponsored in many cities by the Fatherhood Forum in New York, in which fathers and whole families can join in activities designed to expand the range of their positive experiences together. More of these kinds of resources for fathers are listed in the resources section at the end of this book.

It is important to remember that women do not have some sort of intuitive expertise for parenting. Although they may have had more interest in or more practice with children, men can develop these, too. One thing is clear from experience: men who are involved in parenting from the very beginning—throughout pregnancy, delivery, and those crucial first years—are more satisfied parents and say that they would not have missed the experience for anything. Furthermore, the partners of such men are significantly less likely to suffer from postpartum depression, because the major early adjustments are shared, which makes them somewhat easier and much more bearable. When these responsibilities are shared, each parent can know that there will be some help and relief and some time to get away and be the person he or she was before parenthood.

One or both partners may need to explore alternative occupational paths, at least temporarily. If you feel that you have been running too hard in the occupational rat race, this is a good time to reconsider your goals in that regard. Many parents take the opportunity provided by this life change to adjust their work pace or setting so that they have time for other important aspects of their lives, including parenthood. One resource organization that can help—New Ways to Work—is a network of community-based groups that use various names in the twenty-seven cities where they are located but share information on alternative ways to work.[8] These groups can advise you on work sharing (also called job sharing) and other part-time options. They have also helped encourage companies to develop flexible time schedules that allow parents more opportunities to meet their child care needs. A nationwide survey commissioned by the 1980 White House Conference on Families found that the primary concern of most parents was the strains of conflicting work and family demands on their time. The highest priority was to encourage employers to make it easier for working parents to balance these conflicting demands, through such options as flexible work hours, negotiable family leave, and part-time work with the same pay rate, seniority, and other benefits as full-time work of the same type.

Parental leaves, whereby a new parent can take a prolonged unpaid leave but still return to the same position, also seem to be gaining more acceptance. According to a recent survey, however, only 9 percent of the large corporations offer formal unpaid child care leave for fathers. Among the firms that do have such arrangements are American Telephone and Telegraph, Columbia Broadcasting System, Procter & Gamble, and United Airlines. Others, such as Equitable Life, IBM, and Dow Chemical have no formal policy but will allow up to a one-year leave for either parent.

Although this option should be the prerogative of either parent, one of the few thorough books on the subject recognizes current realities in its title: *Managing Your Maternity Leave.*[9] The book's discussion of strategy and timing for both leaving and returning to a job can be useful for men and women. There are detailed discussions of strategy options throughout the leave process, based on the authors' experiences as career consultants who experienced mid-career parenthood themselves, as well as summaries of state laws on leave rights and a directory of state and local fair employment practices agencies. The authors suggest that your strategy of negotiation with your employer be a positive one, based on the following theme:

> I am a valuable employee who loves her job. I want to stay and will do so delightedly, but I need your help in the following areas to allow me to remain in your employ.[10]

Both employee and employer can gain from the process. The employee can arrange necessary concessions, and the company can retain a loyal, motivated, experienced employee, when both sides agree to be as flexible as possible in developing a transition plan that is least costly to both the company and the employee.

If both partners feel that they must return to full-time work as soon as possible, you should begin planning for child care as soon as you confirm pregnancy. There are far fewer child care providers than there are parents in need of them, and the best options always have waiting lists. You will have to be very persistent about child care. It takes time to locate and arrange good caretaking situations, and you must do more than telephone each possibility. Only personal visits (preferably some without advance notice) can show you how they really operate. Furthermore, even the best arrangements have a way of falling apart when you need them most, so backup arrangements are also necessary.

All states, major urban areas, and many other areas now have child care information and referral services that can help you start your search for child care.[11] (See the resources section.) However, the operative word here is "start"; these organizations provide information about services—and often a checklist you can use to begin evaluating them—but they don't provide information about quality or availability. You will have to determine these things yourself. Many successful parents and would-be parents become rather obsessed with this topic, asking everyone they know for leads and evaluations of their experiences. If you continue to work, the subjective quality of your parenting—and, therefore, of your life during the first four or five years of parenthood—can depend more on your success in arranging child care that is satisfactory to you than on any other factor.

Although most parents still use child care options they arrange in their own homes or their home neighborhood, you should not ignore the gradual changes that are occurring with regard to child care in the workplace. Child care is being successfully negotiated as a fringe benefit in both public and private organizations. Some companies provide indirect help, such as referrals or vouchers to help employees with the cost of care. Others support nearby facilities in exchange for priority in placement for company employees. A small proportion of companies support on-site child care facilities; these are the arrangements most preferred by employees, but they are the most expensive alternative for companies.

A recent Harris Poll found that more than two-thirds of the personnel executives surveyed expect child care to become a company benefit within the next five years.[12] Companies are doing this partly to remain competitive in terms of benefits offered but also because they are aware of findings of lower absenteeism, higher morale, and improved public relations in companies that provide child care benefits. There has always been a strong correlation between the availability of child care and patterns of employee absenteeism and turnover, but the awareness of the value of assisting employees with child care has grown with the increasing proportion of women in management and other high-level positions. As more fathers assume an active role in early parenting, perhaps the level of available child care in the United States will begin to approach the levels in European and English commonwealth countries, where readily available child care is regarded as being in everyone's best interests. For the present, however, you should anticipate that the effort and cost of obtaining quality child care will be a major part of your efforts in the early years of parenthood.

Another large-scale issue is how you will handle transitions other than those connected with your work. For example, will you also be planning to move to a more child-oriented living space? The timing and strategy of such changes can also benefit from advance planning. Try to minimize major transitions by sequencing them and by building as much flexibility as you can into the scheduling of each change. All transitions are stressful, but the stress can be made more manageable by preplanning and by spreading out the transitions as much as possible.

Life is not just work and parenthood, although it may seem that way for a while at the beginning. If you are going to preserve your own identity and the adult relationships that are essential to you, you may have to struggle to ensure that you leave some time for them, too. Many marriages face severe strain after the arrival of a child, because no time is spent on nourishing the adult relationship amid the turmoil and exhaustion. You are not likely to have much time for all the other activities you once enjoyed, but any time is better than none. Also, if you are the sort of person who really needs some private time to be alone and recharge your inner resources, don't just give yourself permission to continue doing so—assert the importance of such time for helping you be the person you and those close to you knew before parenthood. You will find the time if you are determined to do so.

You should also think about smaller-scale transitions. Even if you feel prepared to share your life and your partner with a new family member, take the time to consider the pervasive effects this small but very powerful addition will have on your daily life. To get some sense of what this means, make a quick list of how you spent your time in the last twenty-four hours, and do the same for a weekend day and night. How much time in those periods was free time? How much time could you make free? In other words, what is most important to you on a daily basis, and how much of that could be done with unpredictable interruptions? How much of it could be done only when the baby is sleeping? You should realize that some babies don't sleep very much, and you may get one of those. Now take an observant walk around your living space. Of the things you treasure that might be fragile, how many can you put out of the way for the duration of a childhood? How risky is your environment for someone with more curiosity than good sense? If you can come to see the small details of time and space from a child's perspective and adapt things accordingly, you will avoid a great deal of worry and strife.

That, really, is what all of this advice about planning has been about. Parenthood provides joys and worries, but half the trick is to plan ahead so that some of the worries can be avoided and time is allowed for the joys. If you feel that you are already very good at planning and scheduling, my final advice is to be aware that parenthood and scheduling are almost contradictory. Your best and most useful plans will be those that are most flexible, because children are put on this earth to teach us patience and adaptability. If you can accept this paradox and still keep your sense of humor, the riches of parenthood will be much more apparent to you than its costs.

Notes

1. G. Greene, "A Vote Against Motherhood," *Saturday Evening Post,* January 1963, p. 233.

2. E. Peck and J. Senderowitz, *Pronatalism: The Myth of Mom and Apple Pie* (New York: Crowell, 1974); J. Veevers, *Childless by Choice* (Toronto: Butterworth, 1980).

3. Advertisements sponsored by Planned Parenthood of America, described in E. Whelan, *A Baby? . . . Maybe* (New York: Bobbs-Merrill, 1975), pp. 55–56. Similar lists of "wrong reasons" are available from the National Organization for Optional Parenthood (NAOP); see the resources section at the end of this book.

4. G. Hendershot, "Maternal Age and Overdue Conceptions," *American Journal of Public Health* 74 (1984):35–38.

5. A.H. deCherney and G.S. Berkowitz, "Female Fecundity and Age" (editorial), *New England Journal of Medicine* 306 (1982):424–426.

6. "The New Origins of Life" (cover story), *Time,* September 10, 1984.

7. S.A. Sullivan, *The Father's Almanac* (Garden City, N.Y.: Doubleday Dolphin, 1980).

8. See New Ways to Work in the resources section at the end of this book. See also M. Fox, *Put Your Degree to Work* (New York: Norton, 1979).

9. M. Wheatley and M.S. Hirsch, *Managing Your Maternity Leave* (Boston: Houghton Mifflin, 1983).

10. Ibid., p. 59.

11. B. Berger, S. Callahan (eds.), *Child Care and Mediating Structures* (Washington, D.C.: American Institute of Public Policy Research, 1979); K.S. Perry, *Employers and Child Care: Establishing Services through the Workplace* (Washington, D.C.: U.S. Government Printing Office, August 1982).

12. Reported in O. Ornati and C. Buckham, "Day Care: Still Waiting Its Turn as a Standard Benefit," *Management Review* 72 (1983):56–60.

A Personal Postscript

You may be wondering how and why I came to write this book and what decisions I have made about parenthood. If I have done my job well and have presented the parenthood choice in a balanced way, the answers to those questions shouldn't be too obvious. My background and personal history include situations similar to many presented here. My twenties, thirties, and some of my forties were spent in completing advanced degrees and in university teaching and research. There was a great deal to do, and the accomplishments were exciting, challenging, and sometimes difficult and discouraging. I was ambivalent about parenthood, and I still am in many ways.

My own ambivalence arose partly because of my personal experience with the costs of parenthood. I had one child before I was 20 and a broken marriage before I gave birth. As a single parent who had not even finished college, parenthood for me was an endless struggle to pay the bills, continue my education, and still have the time and energy to be both a mother and a father. I wasn't very good at any of this, partly because of chronic exhaustion and inadequate personal and financial resources. My child and I sort of grew up together, without much help, because there were very few child care resources then.

If I had read this book when I was 30 or 40, I would have been in the "no" group, because my life was full and nurturing in many ways, and my career in public health was finally developing as I had wished. At that point, my history of both endometriosis and fibrosis led me to blithely disregard contraception in a new relationship at age 40. Two years later, my husband and I were astounded to be informed that I was pregnant, despite the infertility we had assumed was permanent. Frankly, I greeted the news with very mixed emotions, but my husband was delighted. (I thought he should have known better; after all, he had two children from a previous marriage in college at that point.)

We learned a great deal in a short period of time—about amniocentesis (which was vastly reassuring) and about all of the myths and existing "rules" about parents of our age. For example, thanks, in part, to our efforts, the local hospital no longer automatically excludes parents over 35 from the alternative birth center. Our daughter arrived a bit late but quickly and easily (and naturally), and after two years, we are still enjoying her more than we would have thought possible. She is bright, quick, and perfect, except for an unfortunate tendency to need very little sleep. We are both working less and spending more time with her. Many things just don't get done on time, or at all. My work on this book approached both categories, but I am sure that, from our experiences, it has gained in depth what it lost in promptness.

Resources

This annotated list of resources is divided into the following subject areas:

Adoption

Remaining childless or uncertainty about parenthood

Environmental and occupational exposures and pregnancy

Fatherhood

Genetic counseling and birth defects

Health habits and reproductive health

Infertility

Pregnancy and childbirth

Single parenthood

Work and parenthood

Each of these sections contains information for readers who want to explore the topic in more detail. Included are names and descriptions of organizations that can provide information and, often, support services as well as suggestions for further reading on the topic.

Adoption

Adoption Resource Exchange of North America
67 Irving Place
New York, NY 10003
(212)254-7460

A resource for information exchange about adoption that has extensive information about programs and requirements, with a special focus on adoption of children with special needs.

AASK (Aid to Adoption of Special Kids)
3530 Grand Avenue
Oakland, CA 94610
(415)451-1748

A "no-fee" agency that works with adoption agencies in all areas to help
locate and place special children—older children sibling groups, children of
minority or mixed racial background, and those with physical or emotional
handicaps.

Holt International Children's Service, Inc.
P.O. Box 2880
Eugene, OR 97402

A nonprofit child placement organization; most of its work is in locating
children from other countries.

OURS, Inc. (Organization for a United Response)
3307 Highway 100 North, Suite 302
Minneapolis, MN 55422
(612)535-4829

A voluntary organization of adoptive parents that can provide resource information on all kinds of adoptions, including international and independent
adoption; also publishes a bimonthly newsletter.

World Family Adoptions, Inc.
5048 Fairy Chasm Road
West Bend, WI 43095

An agency that specializes in international adoptions.

Single-Parent Adoptions

SPACE (Single Parents for Adoption of Children Everywhere)
6 Sunshine Avenue
Natick, MA 01760
(617)655-5426

A voluntary parent organization that provides network information for single
adopting parents.

Committee for Single Adoptive Parents
3824 Legation Street, NW
Washington, DC 20015

Further Reading

Plumez, Jacqueline Horner. *Successful Adoption*. New York: Harmony Books, 1982.

A fairly recent, comprehensive guide that discusses all necessary steps in finding and raising adoptive children; covers conventional state agency adoptions as well as independent and international alternatives; also includes an extensive reference and resource section.

Remaining Childless or Uncertainty about Parenthood

National Alliance for Optional Parenthood (NAOP)
2010 Massachusetts Avenue, NW
Washington, DC 20036

National headquarters for an organization with many local chapters; you may find one in your area. The organization was founded to promote a childless choice, but now includes members who are parents and nonparents, single and married. The present goals are to help change the pronatalist and sexist cultural stereotypes that we all live with and to provide support both for those who are certain of their childfree choice and for those who are still uncertain.

American Association for Marriage and Family Therapy
924 West Ninth Street
Upland, CA 91786

An organization of professionals (medical, psychological, and social work) that can provide names of therapists who specialize in family therapy for couples facing major problems or disagreements regarding a parenthood decision.

Association for Voluntary Sterilization
798 Third Avenue
New York, NY 10017

An organization of physicians and others who can provide information about the relative merits and costs of various sterilization options as well as names of cooperating physicians in all areas of the United States.

Further Reading

Peck, E., and Senderowitz, J. (eds.). *Pronatalism: The Myth of Mom and Apple Pie*. New York: Crowell, 1974.

A classic collection of essays and articles on the pervasive and continuing influence of pronatalism in our history and in current policies.

Faux, M. *Childless by Choice: Choosing Childlessness in the 80's*. Garden City, N.Y.: Anchor Press, 1984.

A brief, up-to-date presentation of various aspects of the childless decision, including relationships, costs of children, work and parenthood conflict, and the psychology of motherhood.

Veevers, J. *Childless by Choice*. Toronto: Butterworth, 1980.

The most thorough research discussion of the subject, by a professional who has devoted much of her career to studying childless couples.

Environmental and Occupational Exposures and Pregnancy

National Institute on Occupational Safety and Health (NIOSH)
4676 Columbia Parkway
Cincinnati, OH 45226
(513)684-2427

A federal agency with the responsibility for evaluating working conditions in this country. Its services include sending investigators to workplaces if there are safety concerns and providing resource information from one of the largest reference libraries on the subject.

Women's Occupational Health Resource Center
School of Public Health
Columbia University
60 Haven Avenue, B-1
New York, NY 10032
(212)694-3464

Provides reference and resource materials from its research library.

Note: The following advocacy organizations were formed, at least in part, because their organizers felt that "official" agencies were not doing enough about a particular problem. Their publications should be read with this consideration in mind; in many cases, they have been instrumental in forcing public health action that was long overdue.

DES Action
1638B Haight Street
San Francisco, CA 94117

A national organization with affiliates in thirty states; provides information and support about DES exposure, physician referrals, phone counseling, connection to support groups, and printed resource materials; also publishes a quarterly newsletter, *DES Action Voice*.

Carcinogen Information Center
P.O. Box 6057
St. Louis, MO 63139

A nonprofit advocacy organization that collects information on carcinogenic hazards in the environment, such as radiation, microwave emissions, and other potentially harmful substances; provides free copies of its bulletin, "Carcinogen Information."

Health Right
175 Fifth Avenue
New York, NY 10010

An organization concerned with women's health that publishes a newsletter, pamphlets, and policy papers on various relevant topics.

Further Reading

Heinonen, O.P.; Slone, D.; and Shapiro, S. *Birth Defects and Drugs in Pregnancy.* Littleton, Mass.: Publishing Sciences Group, 1977.

Shepard, T.H. *Catalog of Teratogenic Agents,* 2d ed. Baltimore, Md.: Johns Hopkins University Press, 1976.

Fatherhood

The Fatherhood Project
Bank Street College of Education
610 West 112th Street
New York, NY 10025
(212)663-7200

The broadest and most complete effort to encourage the development of a wide range of options for male involvement in childrearing. Begun in 1981, the project has four major areas of effort: acting as a clearinghouse for options that already exist in the United States; publishing information on these options; developing model programs in father education and support; and participating in efforts to encourage cultural change toward more male nurturing and active participation of fathers in the parenting role. Ten years ago, as director James A. Levine points out, such a project could not have been funded; now it responds to more than 10,000 inquiries per year and sponsors successful "Fatherhood Forums" in many major cities. The project's publications, available from the Bank Street College Bookstore, include *How to Start a Father–Child Group,* a manual based on its own successful weekend program, "Something Special for Dads-and Kids"; *How to Start a Baby-Care Program for Boys and Girls,* another manual based on its own successful experience in teaching children nonsexist child care; and *Fatherhood, U.S.A.,* an extensive resource manual listing and describing hundreds of programs for fathers in health care, education, social and supportive services, legal services, and employment. In spring 1985, the project plans to publish a policy volume on fatherhood and social change, *The Future of Fatherhood.*

Planned Parenthood Federation of America
810 Seventh Avenue
New York, NY 10019
(212)541-7800

Among the many excellent services of this organization is the newsletter *Emphasis,* which has focused on various aspects of the male role in family planning; also provides local resource information through its own clearinghouse, LINK.

Nurturing News
187 Caselli Avenue
San Francisco, CA 94114
(415)861-0847

A newsletter for nurturing men; with reviews of books, films, and other materials and special-focus issues on both the personal and professional lives of men as nurturing persons; published quarterly, $6.00 per year.

Genetic Counseling and Birth Defects

National Foundation—March of Dimes
Genetic Counseling Centers
1275 Mamaroneck Avenue
White Plains, NY 10605
(914)428-7100

An organization with a long history of working to help prevent, diagnose and treat birth defects. One of its activities is encouraging the development of birth defects analysis and counseling centers. The organization can provide information on types of genetic counseling available and the locations nearest to you; there is often a local or state chapter that can also help. In some areas, if health insurance or other funding is not available for someone whose age, family history, or other circumstances make amniocentesis and genetic counseling advisable, the organization can also provide financial assistance.

National Institute on Child Health and Human Development
National Institute of Health
Bethesda, MD 20014

The federal health agency that sponsors most research on genetic disorders and birth defects; publishes an annual report on research it is supporting.

National Clearinghouse for Human Genetic Disease
P.O. Box 28612
Washington, DC 20005

Answers questions from the public and professionals and provides a catalog of resources on genetic disease.

National Information Center for the Handicapped
P.O. Box 1492
Washington, DC 20013

Provides information on various disabilities and listings of appropriate parent support organizations.

National Down Syndrome Society
146 East 57th Street
New York, NY 10022

Disseminates information to parents of children with Down syndrome.

Down's Syndrome Congress
1640 West Roosevelt Road, Room 156 E
Chicago, IL 60608
(312)226-0416

An international organization of parents and professionals; publishes a newsletter ten times a year with information and networking ideas; coordinates parent support groups.

National Capital Tay-Sachs Foundation
P.O. Box 4105
Silver Spring, MD 20904

A nonprofit foundation that supports carrier detection, public education, research, and health care and supportive services to families with an affected child; local chapters around the country.

National Association for Sickle Cell Disease
3460 Wilshire Boulevard, Suite 1012
Los Angeles, CA 90102

An organization that provides educational materials on sickle cell disease and makes referrals to local diagnostic and treatment resources and to local parent support groups.

Further Reading

President's Commission for the Study of Ethical Problems in Medicine and Biomedical and Behavioral Research, *Screening and Counseling for Genetic Conditions: The Ethical, Social, and Legal Implications of Genetic Screening, Counseling, and Education Programs.* Washington, D.C.: U.S. Government Printing Office, February 1983.

A summary, written for the nontechnical reader, of the study of screening and counseling for genetic conditions mandated by Public Law 95-622. The commission considered the use and value of screening and counseling in addition to its current scientific and clinical merits.

Rubin, P. *Its Not Too Late for A Baby: For Men and Women Over 35.* Englewood Cliffs, N.J.: Spectrum Books, 1980.

An excellent book by a genetic counselor at Columbia-Presbyterian Medical Center in New York. The description of genetics and determination of family risk is thorough but nontechnical.

Kessler, S. *Genetic Counseling: Psychological Dimensions.* New York: Academic Press, 1979.

A thorough discussion by the director of the training program in genetic counseling at the University of California, Berkeley.

Milunsky, A. *Know Your Genes.* Boston: Houghton Mifflin, 1977.

Milunsky, A. *The Prenatal Diagnosis of Hereditary Disorders.* Springfield, Ill.: Thomas, 1973.

The first of these books is written for the general reader who has no technical training; the second is for professionals.

Health Habits and Reproductive Health

American Diabetes Association
2 Park Avenue
New York, NY 10016

A physician referral center; offers literature on diabetes and pregnancy and provides information on local chapters.

American Lung Association
1740 Broadway
New York, NY 10019

Provides information on pregnancy and smoking.

National Council on Alcoholism, Inc.
733 Third Avenue
New York, NY 10164

Provides information on drinking and pregnancy and referrals for treatment.

Endometriosis Association
c/o Bread and Roses
Women's Health Center
238 Wisconsin Avenue
Milwaukee, WI 53202

Provides informational brochures on endometriosis.

DES Action
1638B Haight Street
San Francisco, CA 94117

A national organization with affiliates in 30 states; provides information and support about DES exposure, physician referrals, phone counseling, written materials, and support groups; also publishes a quarterly newsletter, *DES Action Voice.*

Society for the Protection of the Unborn through Nutrition (SPUN)
17 North Wabash Avenue
Chicago, IL 60602

Provides training and educational materials on nutrition during pregnancy for parents and professionals and publishes a newsletter that reports and evaluates current research in this area.

Infertility

American Fertility Society
1801 Ninth Avenue South
Birmingham, AL 35205

A society of physicians who specialize in infertility; provides local referrals.

Planned Parenthood of America
810 Seventh Avenue
New York, NY 10019

Although usually considered a resource for contraception, also provides testing and counseling services on infertility. The nearest center can usually be found in your local telephone directory, or write to the address above.

Resolve
P.O. Box 474
Belmont, MA 02178

A national support and information group for individuals and couples dealing with infertility; publishes fact sheets on many subjects related to infertility and a newsletter; also sets up support groups and provides referrals to specialists and adoption services.

Further Reading

Eck-Menning, Barbara. *Infertility: A Guide for the Childless Couple*. Englewood Cliffs, N.J.: Prentice-Hall, 1977.

A comprehensive guide on all aspects of infertility.

Pregnancy and Childbirth

Note: Most pregnancies of older women are well within the normal range, and the following resources can provide information and referrals on alternatives within this normal range. If you have reason to be concerned about a high-risk pregnancy, see the suggestions for further reading at the end of this section. In addition, most teaching hospitals and major medical centers have specialized high-risk pregnancy and delivery units; there should be one near you.

International Childbirth Education Association (ICEA)
P.O. Box 20852
Milwaukee, WI 53220

An organization that provides information and referrals to educational and discussion groups for pregnant and new parents. It also has an extensive and active mailing and resource division that can supply books, pamphlets, films, and other materials on these subjects by mail. Information on available materials can be obtained from its quarterly publication, *Bookmarks Quarterly.*

American Foundation for Maternal and Child Health
30 Beekman Place
New York, NY 10022
(212)759-5910

An organization of professionals concerned with management of the problems of maternity care; sponsors and reviews research and sponsors an annual conference on the topic.

American Academy of Husband-Coached Childbirth
P.O. Box 52224
Sherman Oaks, CA 93143
(312)788-6662

Promotes the Bradley method of natural childbirth; provides instructor training and materials for childbirth education classes.

American Society for Psychoprophylaxis in Obstetrics (ASPO)
1523 L Street, NW
Washington, DC 20005

Promotes the Lamaze method of natural childbirth; provides instructor training and childbirth preparation educational materials, as well as materials for postpartum discussion and exercise groups.

Cooperative Childbirth Network
14 Truesdale Drive
Croton-on-Hudson, NY 10520

A feminist network that provides resources for woman-centered childbirth education; provides educational materials and publishes a newsletter.

Family Centered Childbirth and Parenting
155 West Fourth Street
Fulton, NY 13069

An organization that promotes childbearing as part of a strong marital relationship; trains couples to teach classes together.

LaLeche League International
9616 Minneapolis Avenue
Franklin Park, IL 60131
(312)455-7730

A long-established, highly regarded organization that promotes breastfeeding; holds an annual meeting and publishes a newsletter and pamphlets as well as the popular book, *The Womanly Art of Breastfeeding*. Many local chapters are available to provide help to new and established parents and to provide support for those who are uncertain about their abilities to breastfeed for any reason.

National Association of Parents and Professionals for Safe Alternatives in Childbirth (NAPSAC)
P.O. Box 267
Marble Hill, MO 63764
(314)238-2010

An organization that promotes the establishment of family-centered alternative birth centers and programs in and out of hospitals.

Further Reading

Kappelman, M.M., and Ackerman, P.R. *Parents After Thirty.* New York: Rawson, Wade, 1980.

A refreshingly informal book by a pediatrician and a child psychologist that is full of commonsense discussions of the physical and personal aspects of the major life change known as parenthood; covers the time period from considering parenthood to being the parent of adolescents.

Bing, E., and Colman, L. *Having a Baby After 30: Reassurance and Professional Guidance for Couples Who Waited.* New York: Bantam Books, 1980.

A basic but thorough introduction to the medical and psychological aspects of pregnancy after 30. Unlike many books on this topic, it is addressed to both fathers and mothers.

Rubin, S.P. *It's Not Too Late for a Baby: For Men and Women Over 35.* Englewood Cliffs, N.J.: Prentice-Hall, 1980.

A book by the founder of the genetic counseling service at Columbia-Presbyterian Medical Center, who is also one of the founding members of the National Society for Genetic Counselors. She is a warm and thoughtful writer, able to integrate professional and observational experience into a highly readable book that covers all aspects of "older" pregnancy but is especially thorough on genetic and developmental aspects.

Further Reading on High-Risk Pregnancy

Freeman, R., and Pescar, R. *Safe Delivery: Protecting Your Baby During High Risk Pregnancy.* New York: McGraw-Hill, 1982.

Hales, D., and Creasy, R.K. *New Hope for Problem Pregnancies.* New York: Harper & Row, 1982.

Single Parenthood

Note: Most of the resources available on this topic are addressed to the parent who has become single after becoming a parent, usually through divorce. Thus, they focus on existing but disturbed relationships with other adults and on problems and issues in raising children past the infant stage. You may conclude that both of these areas have little relevance to your present decision making, and in the immediate sense you are correct; remember, however, that if you decide to go ahead with single parenthood, you will eventually be raising a child past infancy. You will also be trying to get along in a social setting that, as time passes, will not consider you different from other single parents.

Parents Without Partners
International Headquarters
7910 Woodmont Avenue, Suite 1000
Washington, DC 20014
(301)654-8850

The largest single-parent organization in the United States and Canada. Local chapters offer discussions, educational programs, and adult and family activities. The international headquarters can give you information about local resources and will also provide a list of the organization's publications on all aspects of single parenthood. The monthly magazine, *The Single Parent,* is included with membership or is available to nonmembers for $7.50 per year.

Single Parent Resource Center
10 West 23rd Street
New York, NY 10010
(212)620-0755

3896 24th Street
San Francisco, CA 94114
(415)821-7058

Local voluntary organizations that provide resources to help single-parent families develop a network of support based on friends, family, and community. Referrals are made for medical, legal, and counseling services, and immediate help with daily needs can be provided.

MOMMA
P.O. Box 567
Venice, CA 90291

A national membership organization for single mothers.

Sisterhood of Black Single Mothers
P.O. Box 155
Brooklyn, NY 11203
(212)638-0413

National Gay Task Force
100 85th Avenue, Suite 1601
New York, NY 10011
(212)741-5800

An organization that provides information on local support resources for gay and lesbian single parents. It also recommends the pamphlet, *A Gay Parent's Legal Guide to Child Custody,* available from the National Lawyers Guild, 558 Capp Street, San Francisco, CA 94110, for $1.00.

SPACE (Single Parents for Adoption of Children Everywhere)
c/o Betsy Burch
6 Sunshine Avenue
Natick, MA 01760
(617)655-5426

Provides networking with other single adopting parents.

Committee for Single Adoptive Parents
3824 Legation Street, NW
Washington, DC 20015

Further Reading

Atlas, S.L. *Single Parenting: A Practical Resource Guide.* Englewood Cliffs, N.J.: Prentice-Hall, 1981.

A book that differs from many books on single parenthood in that it addresses the interests and needs of the nontypical single-parent family—the never-married and the gay or lesbian single parent—in addition to those of the more usual single parent. The author emphasizes a positive perspective on single parenthood for both parent and child and does not view single parenthood as merely a transitional stage between more conventional parenting arrangements.

Levine, J. *Who Will Raise Children? New Options for Fathers (and Mothers)*. New York: Lippincott, 1976.

The seminal book on nontraditional parenting, especially by fathers who are single, work part-time, or are "househusbands." It includes general and personal descriptions of the experiences, problems, and opportunities facing people who assumed what were very unusual parenting roles at the time.

Pogrebin, L.C. *Growing Up Free: Raising Your Child in the 80's*. New York: McGraw-Hill, 1980.

A book that provides advice and encouragement for raising children in a non-sexist, role-free family situation. It also explores sexism in the educational and legal systems as well as in everyday life.

Working and Parenthood

Association of Part Time Professionals
P.O. Box 3632
Alexandria, VA 22302
(703)370-6206

A nonprofit membership organization that informs members of current events and trends in part-time employment, provides career counseling services, organizes job-development presentations to employers, and publishes a monthly newsletter with job listings.

Catalyst
14 East 60th Street
New York, NY 10022
(212)759-9700

A major clearinghouse for information on women and work. It also sponsors descriptive surveys that assess changes and readiness for change among the nation's employers on such topics as maternity and paternity leave and child care options and benefits. Survey results are published in *Catalyst Career and Family Bulletin*.

National Council for Alternative Work Patterns
1925 K Street NW, Suite 308A
Washington, DC 20006
(202)466-4467

Provides information on job sharing and on flexible and part-time employment; also provides current information on firms and government agencies that have flexible, part-time, and job-sharing programs.

New Ways to Work
National Clearinghouse on Job Sharing
149 Ninth Street
San Francisco, CA 94103
(415)552-1000

One of the oldest job sharing organizations, now linked with more than twenty similar groups throughout the country. It will provide current information on available resources if you send a self-addressed, stamped large envelope. It also provides consultation to employers on alternative work options and their benefits and conducts a counseling program and matching program, with free regular orientation sessions.

Working Mother Magazine
230 Park Avenue
New York, NY 10169
(212)551-9500

A magazine, published monthly, that is directed toward the needs of mothers who work inside or outside the home; also publishes useful reference material on child care resources, changes in employment legislation, and similar topics. Subscription address is P.O. Box 10609, Des Moines, IA 50336.

Further Reading

Olmstead, B., and Smith, S. *The Job Sharing Handbook*. New York, Penguin Books, 1982.

A compendium of ideas and resource materials on job sharing and other alternative working options, written by the two founders of the National Clearinghouse on Job Sharing.

Norris, G., and Miller, J.A. *The Working Mother's Complete Handbook*, rev. ed. New York: Plume—New American Library, 1984.

A widely popular book, with sections on the family, especially child care and family work schedules, and career and a new section in the revised edition on "yourself".

Paulson, J.H. *Working Pregnant*. New York: Fawcett/Columbia, 1984.

Begins with an assessment of your readiness to work a baby into your personal and professional life and includes thorough discussions about planning leave, making day care decisions, and balancing working and parenting demands. The sections on health care, nutrition, and exercise are oriented toward continuing working and are both practical and realistic.

Wheatley, M., and Hirsch, M.S. *Managing Your Maternity Leave.* Boston: Houghton Mifflin, 1983.

A thorough, career-oriented discussion of the periods before, during, and after pregnancy; addresses changes of mind and changes of career as options; also includes appendixes on state laws related to pregnancy, state and local fair employment agencies, and child care information and referral services throughout the country.

Glossary

Abruptio Placentae Premature detachment of the placenta from the surface of the uterus, often causing maternal system reactions such as heavy bleeding and shock.

Alphafetoprotein (AFP) A protein produced by the developing fetus and excreted into the amniotic fluid. An elevated AFP level in pregnancy is a sign of fetal distress, especially major neural-tube birth defects or impending abortion or premature birth.

Amniocentesis Removal of a small amount of amniotic fluid for diagnostic purposes. The procedure is performed around the sixteenth week of pregnancy by insertion of a hollow needle through the abdominal wall into the uterus.

Artificial insemination (AI) A procedure in which live sperm from a donor are placed by syringe at the entrance to the cervix at the time of ovulation in the menstrual cycle.

Birth defects Any physical or mental abnormalities present at birth; they may be of genetic or environmental origin.

Cardiovascular Pertaining to the blood circulation system, including the heart as well as the veins and arteries that carry blood throughout the body.

Carrier (genetic) A person who carries a genetic characteristic as part of his or her chromosomes. The characteristic may have no observable signs but can be passed on to the next generation. For example, women can carry the hereditary risk of hemophilia and pass it on to their sons and daughters, but only males demonstrate the disease.

Cervix The area of the lower end of the uterus; the opening between the uterus and vagina that dilates dramatically to permit childbirth.

Cesarean section Surgical delivery of a baby through an incision made in the lower abdominal and uterine walls.

Chorionic villus biopsy Removal of a small portion of tissue from the surface of the chorion (a precursor of the placenta) for diagnostic assessment. The procedure is done at approximately the eighth week of pregnancy by insertion of a catheter into the uterus through the vagina.

Chromosomes Portions of the nucleus of every living cell containing the genetic material that determines hereditary characteristics. Human cells, except for egg and sperm cells, have forty-six chromosomes each; the reproductive cells have twenty-three chromosomes each and combine at conception to total forty-six.

Cohort A population group, with one or more common characteristics, that is usually studied over a period of time (for example, women born between 1940 and 1945, college graduates).

Congenital Pertaining to a characteristic that is present at birth. Congenital defects are abnormalities that may have hereditary and/or environmental causes.

Diabetes An abnormality in the body's ability to produce insulin and, therefore, to process sugars. Age at onset and severity have both genetic and environmental components.

Diethylstilbestrol (DES) A synthetic estrogen hormone often used in the 1950s and 1960s to prevent threatened abortion in early pregnancy. Its use has been linked with vaginal cancer and other abnormalities of the reproductive system in male and female offspring of women who were given the hormone during their pregnancies.

Diseases of aging. Conditions that become more prevalent in the population with increasing age, including, most commonly, hypertension, arthritis, adult-onset diabetes, and emphysema.

Dizygotic Pertaining to a multiple birth originating from two fertilized eggs. Because multiple births of this kind occur from two separate conceptions, the offspring may vary as much as any two or more siblings born to the same parents. (Also referred to as fraternal of nonidentical twins.)

Down syndrome (mongolism, or trisomy 21) A chromosomal abnormality in which a child is born with three number 21 chromosomes instead of the usual two. It is associated with mental retardation and a distinctive combination of physical abnormalities.

Eclampsia Convulsions and coma occurring at the end of pregnancy or soon after delivery. Warning signs (preeclampsia or toxemia) include high blood pressure, sudden weight gain due to edema, and protein in the urine.

Ectopic pregnancy Abnormal implantation or attachment of the embryo outside the uterus. The most common site is within a fallopian tube (tubal pregnancy), but implantation can occur elsewhere in the abdomen.

Edema Swelling of any part of the body as a result of excessive accumulation of fluid.

Embryo An unborn child from the first to the eighth week of pregnancy, after which it is called a fetus.

Endometriosis The presence of endometrial tissue (tissue that normally lines the interior of the uterus) elsewhere in the abdomen. The tissue can adhere to and block normal functioning of other organs, such as the ovaries and fallopian tubes, causing infertility.

Epidemiology Study of the distribution of disease and disability in populations and their origin and prevention.

Fallopian tubes The portions of the female reproductive system through which an egg passes en route from the ovary, where it is formed, to the uterus, where implantation normally occurs.

Fecundability The ability to produce offspring.

Fetal alcohol syndrome A combination of birth defects that are characteristic of some infants born to mothers who have a history of heavy alcohol use.

Fetus   An unborn child from the eighth week of pregnancy until birth; prior to eight weeks, it is called an embryo.

Fibroids (fibromyomas or leiomyomas)   Benign growths in the uterus that are composed of fibrous and muscle tissue; they occur more frequently in older women.

Genetic   Hereditary, or from the genes; used in reference to hereditary units located on chromosomes and passed to the offspring from both parents.

Gestation   The duration of a pregnancy, expressed in weeks, calculated from the first day of the last menstrual period.

Heart disease (cardiovascular disease)   Disorders affecting the circulatory system. The most common of such diseases in adults are hypertension and heart failure (evidenced by shortness of breath and swelling of the ankles).

Hemophilia   A sex-linked hereditary disease in which the blood of affected males is incapable of clotting normally.

Hereditary   Occurring through genetic determination; that is, passed from parents to offspring.

Hypertension   Sustained high blood pressure.

Hypoglycemia   Low blood sugar levels.

Infertility   For a man, the inability to cause pregnancy; for a woman, the inability to become pregnant or successfully complete a pregnancy.

Intrauterine growth rate   The normal rate of growth for a fetus during gestation. A fetus whose growth rate is below normal is termed small for gestational age (SGA).

Mongolism   See *Down syndrome.*

Monozygotic   Pertaining to multiple birth resulting from unusual division of cells, immediately after a single conception, into two embryos instead of one; the offspring are always of the same sex and have identical chromosomes. (Also referred to as identical twins.)

Morbidity   Disease, illness, or injury.

Mutagen   Any substance or circumstance that is capable of causing mutation or change in genetic material.

Perinatal   Referring to the time period around (*peri*) birth (*natal*), ranging from the twenty-eighth week of gestation to four weeks after birth.

Placenta   A permeable, spongy structure that attaches the embryo to the wall of the uterus. It provides for the passage of oxygen and nutrients to the fetus and the removal of waste products from the fetus via the umbilical cord. The placenta is expelled as the final part of the birth process (afterbirth).

Placenta praevia   Attachment of the placenta low in the uterus. It may not cause problems, but if it blocks the cervical opening, complications, including hemorrhage, can occur late in pregnancy.

Premature   Referring to birth prior to the fortieth week of gestation or to an infant who is born weighing less than 2,500 grams (about 5.5 pounds) or whose body functions are not yet completely ready to sustain survival successfully.

Prenatal   Referring to the period of gestation, from conception to delivery.

Proteinuria   Excessive protein in the urine; in pregnancy, a sign of preeclampsia.

Risk factor   Any characteristic that is found to be statistically associated with increased likelihood of a specific disease.

Rubella (German measles)   A highly contagious viral infection. Contracting it during early pregnancy can cause a syndrome of major birth defects.

SGA (Small for gestational age)   Referring to a fetus or infant who is smaller than normal at a specific stage of development. The condition can be caused by anything that reduces the ability of the fetus to obtain adequate nutrition and oxygen, including maternal smoking and inadequate weight gain.

Sickle cell disease (sickle cell anemia)   A hereditary condition characterized by sickle-shaped red blood cells and impaired red blood cell function.

Sonography   See *ultrasound.*

Spina bifida   A defect in the spinal column that occurs during early fetal neural-tube development. It is the most common of the neural-tube birth defects, ranging in severity from minor to severe enough to cause perinatal death.

Spontaneous abortion (miscarriage, fetal loss)   Premature expulsion of an embryo or fetus at an early stage of pregnancy, before survival outside the womb is possible.

Syndrome   A group of symptoms or signs that, occurring together, indicate the diagnosis of a specific disease (for example, rubella syndrome, fetal alcohol syndrome).

Tay-Sachs disease   A hereditary deficiency in the essential enzyme hexosaminidase A, leading to neurological deterioration and death of affected infants early in life.

Teratogen   Any substance that is capable of causing damage to an individual or a developing fetus.

Testes   The male gonads, or reproductive glands, which produce hormones and sperm cells.

Torch   Maternal testing for the following diseases that are dangerous to the fetus: toxoplasmosis, rubella, cytomegalovirus, and herpes virus.

Toxemia   See *eclampsia.*

Toxoplasmosis   A serious disease caused by the parasite Toxoplasma; contracted during pregnancy, it can be teratogenic to the fetus.

Trisomy 21   See *Down syndrome.*

Tubal ligation   Surgical cutting or clamping of the fallopian tubes. It is the most common type of permanent sterilization procedure for women.

Ultrasound (sonography)   A diagnostic procedure in which high-frequency sound waves transmitted through a transducer are moved over the skin surface; differences in internal density produce images on a videoscreen, which are photographed and used for diagnostic purposes.

Uterus (womb)   The female reproductive organ, in which an embryo implants and develops throughout gestation.

Vascular   Pertaining to the circulatory system.

Vas deferens   The tubes that carry sperm from the testes to the seminal vesicles, where they are stored in preparation for ejaculation.

Vasectomy   Surgical cutting of the vas deferens. If it is done on both sides, the man is sterile but does not lose sexual ability or interest.

Index

About the Author

Epidemiologist and sociologist **Judith Blackfield Cohen, M.P.H., Ph.D.,** is presently a research epidemiologist in the Department of Medicine at the University of California, San Francisco. She has taught and conducted research in the public health field for 20 years, where her research has included a wide variety of studies directed at understanding the effects of peoples' cultural and psychological circumstances on their risks of health and disease. Although she has published extensively in professional journals on the subjects of Type A behavior and on stress and coping, this is her first book. She completed her degrees in sociology, public health, and epidemiology at the University of California at Berkeley.

July 11

6 38 5 828